Customer Service
Cliff Robison

Rock and Fire Press
Salinas, CA

Customer Service
© 2021 by Cliff Robison

All Rights Reserved.
No portion of this work may be reproduced in any form or by any means without the prior written permission of the author, except for brief excerpts in reviews and criticism. While every effort has been made to ensure accuracy, the author and the publisher take no responsibility for errors or omissions, nor for any cause arising from reliance upon statements of fact found herein.

Cover Photo © 2021 by Janet Thompson
All Rights Reserved.

Library of Congress Catalog Number:

ISBN-13:
978-1-949005-14-1 (print)
978-1-949005-15-8 (eBook)
FIRST EDITION
First Printing

Rock and Fire Press
Salinas, CA

Acknowledgements

Many individuals contributed information, or wisdom, or both, to the writing of this book. There may still be errors herein, of fact, logic, or style, despite the best efforts of those listed below.
For those errors, the author is solely responsible.

Notes regarding the Cover Photo:
Despite my efforts at obfuscation, it is possible that the astute reader may discern the franchise depicted, or possibly even the specific customer service agent.

That franchise, that store, and that agent have always epitomized good service, at least towards me. That is not (lest anyone should wonder) the store known herein as "FEARER TAGOE."

I heartily recommend the chain, the store, and the customer service agent seen on the cover, and am willing to be a reference for any of the above at any point in the future.

DISCLAIMER:

This book contains many thoughts and many opinions.
In matters of fact, every effort has been made to be accurate, but the writer and the publishers take no responsibility for any perceived slight, nor umbrage taken, by any person, establishment, or organization. Opinions expressed are those of the writer, and may or may not reflect reality as we know it.
Actual mileage may vary.

N*I*A*C*IN denies any involvement.

Introduction:
FEARER TAGOE?

THERE'S A FAST-FOOD place not far from my house. I sometimes call it Fearer Tagoe. That's not its name. It's what one of the counter-help used to scream at me when I would try to order.

Don't get me wrong. I'm not down on fast food. I have eaten, and do regularly eat, in restaurants across the spectrum, from fast food to white-table-cloth fine-dining places. And across the board, some have great service and some need a lot of help. That is part of what inspired me to write this book.

Of course, you are wondering what qualifies me to write about customer service. I have spent decades in the hospitality industry. I started as a hotel employee in 1989. I have been the guy who goes to the guestroom and changes the burned-out light bulb. I have been the manager who explains why the light bulb burned out in the first place. I have been the senior manager who explains why I can't honor a verbal offer of a half-price rate, with no confirmation number, on a sold-out weekend when every guestroom in town is booked.

I've stayed in hotels and eaten in restaurants where I was treated like a king. And I've eaten in restaurants where my presence was barely tolerated, even though I'm an undemanding customer and tip very well. The former businesses have earned my repeat business. The latter businesses have not.

I haven't always worked in hotels. I'm also done installation, sales, and maintenance of electronic systems. I've provided technical support. I've worked as a contractor. And all of these have a common factor: Guest contact, also known as customer service.

All of that experience has led me to discover three undeniable rules of customer service:

1. Customers like good service.
2. Customers will pay for good service.
3. Customers will return if they get good service.

These may seem like no-brainers. They may seem so glaringly obvious that you're wondering why I'm bothering to recite them. Well, here's the answer: They are not glaringly obvious.

How do I know? Simple: FEARER TAGOE!

I would innocently walk into the Fearer Tagoe! restaurant, having forgotten my previous experience. I would decide what I wanted, while standing in line. And then I would step up to the register as the previous customer stepped away. So far, so good.

Here's where it all unraveled: When I would start to speak, the counter help would shout "FEARER TAGOE!" at me. I would stop, blink, and recompose myself. This entire time, the counter person would stand perfectly still, staring at me. And again, as soon as I spoke a single syllable, "FEARER TAGOE!"

The second time came as less of a shock, of course. Knowing that the person had shouted at me the first time made me almost expect them to shout again. But it still annoyed me, for three reasons. First, the counter help did not have the courtesy to enunciate the question, "Will this order be for here or to go?"

Secondly, there was plenty of time to pre-empt my order before I began speaking, and to politely ask the question. It was not necessary to wait until I was already speaking to shout over me. Finally, had the counter person simply listened to my order, I would have provided all of the necessary information.

You will be pleased to know that I resisted the urge to shout back. I resisted the urge to give a loud lecture on proper customer service. And I resisted the urge to shout for the manager so that I could yell at both of them. I simply answered the question, and proceeded to place my order in the only manner that was allowed.

You might be thinking that she was trained that way. No doubt, that's true. But it doesn't excuse it. You might be thinking that he couldn't remember the order long enough to punch it in, perhaps that's true as well. It still doesn't excuse it.

Neither explanation excuses poor customer service. There are individual waiters who perform better than the entire rest of the restaurant, despite having received the exact same training. There are waiters who can remember an entire table's orders, both as she relays it to the kitchen and as he delivers it back to the table. In either case, listening politely and *then* asking the programmed questions would be a much better solution than to shout "FEARER TAGOE!"

Here's a general tip: Never shout at a customer.

Here's another: Never interrupt a customer who is speaking.

One last tip before we leave the story: A customer will forgive polite incompetence – for example, having to ask again if that was for here or to go – but will never forgive rudeness. If you have to keep asking questions, but you are polite, the guest will be patient with you, at least to a degree. But if you are rude, it is very likely that they will lose their patience and be rude back to you.

Of course, there are exceptions. There are places where the entire shtick consists of being rude to the customers. In one semi-famous Eagle Rock lunch counter, the counterman always asked "WHADDAYA WANT?" and the only acceptable response was "FOOD!" Any other answer, including "Can I see a menu?" would be met with verbal abuse, to the amusement of the regulars.

There's a BBQ place in Texas, where approaching the front counter at all will result in "WHADDAYA WANT WHADDAYA WANT?" until you shout your order back to them. There are also restaurants with waiters that make it a habit to cut off customers' ties. And so forth.

These are the exceptions. These are places that have made rudeness their distinguishing shtick. People who love these places love them because they can take their friends to see the friends' reactions. For those places, it works, after a manner of speaking, because it's different and because the customer still knows what to expect. But it won't work for everyone.

That is definitely not how to run a restaurant if you're not just trying to make a cheap novelty trick. If you are serious about hospitality, you need to do much better than that.

We'll talk about the customer experience in this book. We'll talk about how to deal with rude customers. We'll talk about food service. We'll talk about other forms of service. We'll talk about design models, and service models. We'll discuss a lot of horror stories about poor service, and we'll talk about great service as well.

If you are involved in any way with customer service, you should be able to get something out of this book. You might even find the secrets that will save your restaurant, hotel, or other business from an early demise.

Chapter One:
How to Speak to Customers

So there I was, in a glass elevator with several guests and the security guard. It was opening night, the grand opening of the hotel, and the lobby was filled with guests who had come to see the twelve-story atrium with a four-story water feature and glass-sided elevators.

And as soon as the elevator doors closed, the control panel went dark and the elevator dropped three feet, leaving us surrounded by staring guests. It was a bit like being in a fishbowl. A crowded fishbowl.

One of the guests in the elevator was an older Korean man who spoke no English. His daughter informed me that he was becoming very agitated, and that he was worried about having enough air to breathe.

I calmly told her that I could feel a draft near the door, that the elevator car was well ventilated, and that people were working to get us out at that very moment. She retorted that her father couldn't understand that, as he only spoke Korean. So I gently asked if she would be so kind as to relay that information to him.

At about that time, my radio informed me that there was a "Code 11" at elevator number one. Code 11 was our code-word for a problem involving an elevator. I had to quietly tell the dispatcher that I was aware of it, as I was inside the elevator car.

Fortunately, the elevator installers were still in house — they had been completing finishing touches on the elevators for days — and one of them was able to open the door from the outside and set us free. It was a very humiliating experience, to say the least.

I can think of a few things I could have done better. I could have turned off my radio, so that guests would not be further infuriated by hearing the dispatcher call me, when I could obviously do nothing to help. I could have gotten the customers in the elevator to see the amusing side of things (though that one would have been a tough sell).

There are also things I could have done worse. I could have been rude to the elderly man's daughter. I could have acted superior and given people orders to calm down and knock off the complaining. I could have shouted at the dispatcher when she asked me to go let people out of the elevator.

In general, I followed the rules for how to speak to a customer.

RULE 1: A customer is always "Sir" or "Madam." Whenever one speaks to a guest, one always says "Yes, Sir," or "Yes, Ma'am," or the equivalent.

There may be minor exceptions. On one occasion, a guest asked me to let him back into his room, as his daughter had locked the keys inside. I explained that I could certainly fulfill his request, but that first I would need to see identification. When he showed me a passport from Germany, I noted the picture (it was him) and the name. I couldn't easily pronounce the last name, so I said, "Vielin danke, Herr Ulrich," and opened the door for him.

Calling the customer by his first name was wrong. I should have used his last name. Unfortunately, I couldn't pronounce it. But by adding the title "Herr" in front of the first name, it became an acceptable, if slightly odd, substitute. I used his name in order to subtly emphasize that I had checked it, and to suggest that I would verify it.

We should probably deal with an important point here: If you are not comfortable saying "Sir" and "Ma'am" or "Mr." or "Ms." or "Mrs." then you may wish to rethink your chosen profession. If, and only if, you can realize that it does not diminish you to be polite, then customer service is a good fit for you.

Let's pause to think about this. Does anything that someone says to me diminish who I am? No, obviously not. If I speak to someone politely, does that diminish who I am? No, obviously not. So if speaking softly and politely will make things flow more easily, and it costs me nothing, why shouldn't I be polite and speak gently?

As an example of poor name usage, please consider this story:

I was once eating in restaurant and I noticed that an elderly man at another table was wearing a ball cap with a USMC logo and the word RETIRED in large letters. The young woman waiting on that table kept referring to that man as "Sweetie," and calling his wife "Dearie." Her condescending tone made me very angry.

As I often do, I held my tongue. What I wanted to say to her was that the gentleman was a hero, and that she owed him far more respect than she was showing. His name was not "Sweetie," and his wife was not "Dearie." They were "Sir" and "Madam."

But I held my tongue. I wrote it off as ignorance. The next time I was there, the young woman was not. I have never seen her again. It might – might – have been because of her poor customer service skills.

RULE 2: "Please" and "Thank you" are mandatory.

Never ask anything of a customer without saying "Please," and never receive anything from a customer without saying "Thank you." In the case of Herr Ulrich, above, I first thanked him for showing me his passport, and then used his name with an appropriate title.

Vielen Danke is the middle ground of German-language thanks, with a bare "Danke" being the least formal, and "Danke-Schoen" being the most. In this case, it was the appropriate one to use. Speaking to Herr Ulrich in German, with the very few words I know in that language, was a simple detail to help him feel at ease, even though he was clearly feeling a bit silly and stressed about the keys.

There are other words that are important in your customer service vocabulary. "Unfortunately" is a word that should precede any bad news. "Unfortunately, I will need to see your passport before I open your room" would be an appropriate usage.

"For your safety" should precede any request that involves a safety concern or a regulation. For your safety, I must ask that you don't swing from the chandelier. For your safety, I will need to ask that you step back from the ledge. For your safety, please take your head out of that lion's mouth. And so on.

"I have to ask" and variations of this phrase will general soften a request. "I'm sorry, Ma'am, but I must ask that you not smoke so close to the front doors. It's the law, unfortunately." "I'm sorry, Sir, but I'm going to have to ask you to leave. You've had too much to drink, Sir."

"Certainly" is an excellent response to any request. Will I send extra towels to your room? "Certainly, Sir!" Will I find reservations for you? "Certainly, Ma'am!"

"How may I help you?" is another great phrase. It's amazingly useful, especially with a friendly smile and a soft tone.

RULE 3: There are No Problems.

Do not ever respond with the phrase, "No problem." If a guest should thank you for something, do not say, "No problem." As endless customer service guides have pointed out, "No problem" begins with a negation and then mentions a problem. It is far better to say, "My pleasure" or some equivalent. "It was my pleasure to serve you, Sir." "It is my pleasure to hold the door for you, Madam."

The curious side effect of saying "My pleasure!" in response to light praise or thanks from others is that you will soon come to be thought of as a very polite individual in your private life, as well.

Now, let's examine a case where proper customer service speech habits could have made all the difference in the world:

One of my friends went to eat at a local place that had excellent local reviews. He had the misfortune to arrive just as they were about to close from lunch and prepare for dinner. His first question, whether they were still open, was pre-empted by a shout of "We're closed!"

Well, he might be able to come back for dinner, at least.

"Yes," he said, "But when – "

"WE'RE CLOSED!"

"When do you re-open?"

"WE'RE CLOSED!"

"ARE YOU OPEN FOR DINNER TONIGHT?" He finally shouted, his face turning red.

"Yeah, we open at six," the employee grudgingly admitted.

I know what you're thinking: FEARER TAGOE! all over again. And you are correct. This proves that poor customer service is not merely limited to a certain fast food place near me.

So how should this have gone?

On seeing him, the restauranteur might have said, "I'm sorry, Sir, but we're just closing."

To which the prospective customer might have said, "When will you be open for dinner?" and on hearing that it would be six that evening, he might have returned later and that might have become his favorite place to eat.

Better still, "Sorry, we're closing, but we'll be open for dinner tonight at six!" No hard feelings, no shouting, no rudeness.

As it is, that man never set foot there again.

Never be rude to a guest. Never shout. Never cut off what a guest is trying to ask you. There is no excuse for any of these things.

I don't want you to think that only restaurants ever have rude workers. That just seems to be where I notice it the most. But it happens other places as well, and the same principles apply.

I was in a drugstore once, at the register to purchase a couple of small items. I happened to have a small piece of trash in my hand, unrelated to any transaction.

"Excuse me," I said to the clerk. "Do you have a receptacle back there for this?"

"Yes, Sir," he said, glaring at me. He pointed through the window, to trash cans on the sidewalk outside. "We keep them out there."

I held my tongue. I did not walk out of the store. I did not call for the manager. And I did not return to that store. Ever.

Another quick tip: Don't be sarcastic. It's rude.

In replaying that event, I probably should have said, "Wrong answer, Smart Aleck. The correct answer is, 'No, Sir, I do not.' Now would you like to try again, or shall I have your manager explain proper customer service to you?"

But I did not. And I did not go back. This leads me to another important point:

RULE 4: Your tone is as important as your words.

There used to be a humorous video on the internet in which two people carried on an entire conversation by saying "Dude!" to each other. Beneath them, subtitles would say things such as "Hi, how are you?" "Hey, don't do that," "Wow, that's cool!" or "I am so disappointed in you right now." The difference in all of these meanings was conveyed by the tone and inflection of the speaker.

In the same way, "We're closed" can be a simple statement of fact, an apology, or a slap in the face, all depending upon the tone and inflection. People sometimes even exploit this by pretending that everything they say should be taken at face value, while everything that is said to them must be taken in the rudest possible context.

We want to do the opposite. We want to be very sensitive and careful when speaking to others, while ignoring any offensive inflection in what others say. We need to meet sarcasm and even outright rudeness with polite, calm, and measured responses.

Again: Nothing that anyone says to me will change who I am. If I understand that, I can be calm when others are not. But what I say to others will affect how they feel, and it costs me nothing to be polite.

I remember one occasion, when I was the Manager on Duty for a certain hotel, and I found a front desk staff in the basement crying. When I asked what was wrong, it turned out that a guest had gotten very angry and very rude. The staff person had answered the guest politely and professionally, and then had come down to the basement to recompose herself. She did everything exactly right.

We will discuss angry customers in a later chapter.

On this particular situation, I thanked the staff member for being professional and for wisely knowing when to take a time-out. Then I went to the lobby and politely spoke to the guest. It turns out that the matter at hand – the thing that made the guest angry and impatient – had nothing to do with the hotel at all.

The staff member, by using the correct tone of voice, was able to defuse the situation and bring it to a peaceful resolution. What you say is important, but the way in which you say it can sometimes be even more important.

    Maintain a polite tone at all times. Speak politely. Be polite. Kill them with kindness. Make it a game to be as polite to them as they are rude to you.

Chapter Two
How to Be the Best Restaurant Server in the World.

ONE EVENING, A FRIEND and I had been working late, and when we finally tried to have a bite of supper, we found, to our dismay, that most of our favorite restaurants were closed for the evening. One restaurant, despite being practically empty, told us that they had no tables. Others, even though they were supposedly open for hours yet, were closing early, or only taking orders to go.

At last, we tried one final restaurant before resorting to fast food. And we had the best service ever.

The waiter that night – and I still remember that his name was Andrew, which should tell you how memorably impressive the service was – was friendly without being familiar, and attentive without being intrusive. He assured us that the kitchen was still open, took our orders quickly and accurately, and brought us a very welcome basket of rolls.

Our drinks came quickly, and he made sure that they were never empty. It was as if they simply refilled themselves. A truly professional waiter is almost invisible. He or she will simply get things done without drawing attention.

When he brought our food, or when he stopped to ask if we needed anything, he always stepped into our field of vision and gave us a moment to end our sentences before speaking.

The food was good, but as the old saying goes, hunger is the best sauce. I have forgotten the meal, but I still remember the excellent and professional service that we received. To this day, when the subject of customer service comes up in conversation, that friend will ask me, "Remember Andrew?"

Not only did we tip well, but I also went out of my way to write a letter to the manager of that restaurant, commending that waiter by name. By the way, comment cards are nice, and online surveys will get kudos from the manager. But to make a real impression, an actual snail-mail postal letter tops them all. It is certain to be pinned up in the kitchen for all of the staff to see. The waiter will be a hero to his or her peers and to the manager. It never hurts to speak well of someone, and especially if you have clearly gone out of your way to do it.

So, let's talk about all the things that Andrew did right.

First, he made us feel welcome. He assured us that the kitchen was still open, that we were not too late, that we were not a burden, and that he would gladly serve us dinner. He didn't say all of those things verbally; he said most of those things through his tone and his attitude.

Second, he saw the priorities. He knew that we were hungry, and took our drink orders quickly. He brought us rolls quickly. After we ordered, he made sure that our orders got to the kitchen, and that as soon as they were ready, they came straight to the table.

Third, he wasn't intrusive. There are two extremes for waitstaff. One is to hover over the table, constantly asking if there's anything that's needed. The other extreme is to vanish into the kitchen and never be seen again. Andrew struck a perfect balance. He did appear at our table from time to time, but most often he simply kept an eye on us and did what was necessary. When my glass became empty, a full one appeared almost magically. Later, the empty one that I placed near the edge of the table simply vanished into thin air.

What Andrew clearly understood was that we were not there for witty conversation. We were not there to create a fun experience. We were not there to meet new people. We were there because we were hungry, and because we wanted to converse with each other over dinner.

The cardinal sin for intrusive behavior is for the customer to be in mid-sentence when the server, completely unannounced, shouts from behind the customer's elbow, "Everything good here? You guys need anything?"

Instead, when checking on a customer's table, first step into the field of vision. Never speak from behind a customer who doesn't know that you're there. It's startling, not to mention rude.

Next, pause so that the customer can finish the sentence before you speak. Wait for the customer to look at you. If necessary, softly clear your throat to attract their attention. Then, and only then, ask if the customer has everything necessary to enjoy the meal.

This also applies when the customer has her mouth full. If you step into the field of vision, the customer will have a moment to chew and swallow instead of choking on their food while trying to respond to you.

> **A**pproach and be seen.
> **B**efore speaking, wait for a pause.
> **C**asually ask any question that you may have.

Does it take a moment more? Yes. Will it make you slow down? Yes. But is it proper customer service? Yes. There's a cliché that you will hear in the customer service industry. It goes, "The customer is not an interruption to our business. The customer is our business."

And that's true.

The opposite failure is to vanish. You should never be away from an active table for more than a few minutes. There are things that will call you away – side work, checking on an order in the kitchen, taking a break as required by labor law. But if you are going to be away from the table for more than a couple of minutes, you need to have another server cover for you. You do not need to bring the other server over and introduce them – that was a fashionable, if annoying, practice in some places for a while, but it has thankfully declined into obscurity.

A couple of remarkable examples of the vanishing waiter stand out in my memory. I once stopped with some friends at a family-style restaurant for breakfast. We were seated in a room that was nearly full, and as we decided on our orders and lowered our menus, we became aware of an odd fact – no one in the room was eating. Every table was waiting for a waiter to come and take drink orders. Every. Single. One.

A family got up and walked out, and as they passed by the table, one of my friends asked, "Excuse me – how long were you waiting?"

The answer was unprintable, but in paraphrase, he said, "Far too long."

We soon discovered that the waiter covering that room had reached the end of her shift, had not been relieved by an oncoming waiter, and had simply left. The hostess hadn't noticed, and was unaware that she was filling a room with customers who would wait forever.

Yes, the hostess should have caught on quicker. Yes, an on-the-ball manager could have realized that there was a staffing issue. Yes, the waiter had a right to leave at the end of her shift. But the very least that she might have done was to say, "I'm off and I have to leave, but my relief didn't show, so someone needs to cover."

Remember that the cardinal rule of customer service is to treat customers as you want to be treated. I am fairly certain that the vanishing waiter would have wished for someone to tell the hostess, had she been the customer. But she did not exercise that same courtesy.

The other time that I strongly remember a vanishing waiter was in a certain Thai restaurant. Thai food tends to be extremely spicy, so you will probably want water in addition to whatever beverage you are drinking.

Some friends and I were midway through a meal when we flagged down the waiter and asked for more water. The spices had exceeded our beverages. The waiter acknowledged the request and promptly vanished.

I am fairly certain that he was not abducted by aliens, because he did reappear some twenty-five minutes later, when he brought both the check and the water. I suppose that a twenty-five minute wait might be appropriate if you are forced to make the water yourself, perhaps by burning hydrogen gas in an oxidizing flame. But in any other case – and especially when waiting tables in a Thai restaurant – it is inexcusable.

Neither I, nor any of those friends, have ever returned to that place. And we have been very vocal in telling others why we don't eat there.

Inattentiveness doesn't have to be from apathy or distraction. There was a restaurant in my town where once of the servers was always in a hurry. She hustled from one end of the dining room to the other, her eyes fixed on her target. She raced from one place to another, always busy, always getting things done.

The problem was that she ignored all the customers in between. She was so focussed on one task that she lost track of all of the others. It was nearly impossible to flag her down for service.

Don't get me wrong: It's not easy to wait on an entire room all by yourself. Even with a couple of people covering a zone, it can be a bit crazy. Still, you need to have an alert eye. Scan the room from time to time. Make a point of coming to a complete stop, and looking at each table for which you have responsibility. Look for empty glasses that need to be refilled. Look for guests who are staring at you (that's a very strong hint that they need something). Look for guests who are not eating, or staring at their food, or looking around for something.

That's the attentive part. Remember the old saying: "Slow is smooth and smooth is fast." Slow down and see the big picture. See the entire room. Then, casually, efficiently, and methodically, see to each of the tables.

On the other side of the coin, there is a restaurant in a neighboring town that is staffed by an elderly Lebanese man. He seats the guests, he takes their orders, he cooks the food, and he serves the food. In the end, he takes the check as well.

This one man is able to remain in constant motion because he is efficient. He has a method, and he works through his method. Seat this guest, take that order, bring drinks for these guests, check that sauce, serve this plate, seat that guest, and take this order. It's actually quite impressive, and it's exactly the opposite of the server who races from end to end. One expends a lot of energy and wastes a lot of effort; the other uses just the right amount of energy and makes just the right effort.

Attentive, but not intrusive.

Next, we need to be friendly, but not familiar. The customer is not your friend; the customer is not your enemy. You need to put aside any feeling that you might have and be entirely professional.

I've been to restaurants where the waiter actually slid into the booth and sat there while she wrote down the orders. That is a bit too far on the familiar side. I've also been to restaurants where the waiter acted like asking for service was a serious inconvenience to her. That is a bit too far on the unfriendly side. A good balance is needed.

In the category of "not friendly enough," I am reminded of an incident in which two brothers (from a family that shall remain nameless) visited a family restaurant for a late night snack over coffee. To their dismay, the waiter was a young woman with whom one of the brothers had a mutual dislike. I cannot condone the young woman's attitude, or the brothers' response.

She, for her part in this event, should have ignored who they were and concentrated on the task at hand. Had she acted professionally, the rest of the incident might have been avoided. But she instead acted as if it were beneath her to wait on them, and as if she was only doing so because she was required by her job.

The brothers, to their credit, left a tip. However, it was entirely in coins, and it was left inside an inverted water glass full of water. As they left, she watched them from the bussing station and shouted, "I saw what you did!"

See how this sort of unprofessional behavior simply cascades? Had I managed that establishment, it would have been her last night there. The two brothers would have been placed on notice that similar tricks would have them barred from entry in the future (Yes, it is sometimes okay to 86 a customer, but that is the manager's call, not yours).

That's an extreme case. It's probably not a good example. And if it ever happens to you, simply carry a bus tub to the table, place it under the edge of the table, then slide the entire glass off the edge of the table into the bus tub. Then you can retrieve the coins without making a mess.

There's an equal and opposite over-reaction, and that is to be overly friendly, or even flirtatious. Flirting may work to your advantage, and may get big tips. But those tips come at a price, usually the job itself. Don't get me wrong: If you know a customer and have a long history with him, there's nothing wrong with using his name. You might even chat about something that you have in common.

But calling a stranger by her name would be completely different. Chatting about your personal issues with a stranger is simply out of the question. Discussing your family, your childhood, your future plans – all of those are beyond the scope of a professional demeanor.

In one hotel, I had a night maintenance worker who sometimes had trouble finding the boundary. I had to speak to him often about being professional in his speech. We received several comment cards in which the guest mentioned the extent of the things he had told them: Details of his family life, of his aspirations, of his work schedule, of his recent vacations. Some guests found it amusing, and others burdensome.

During one of my conversations with him, he defended his statements on the ground that they were true, and that he was simply "being honest" with the guests. Did I want him to lie to the guests?

I asked him, "Suppose that there was a guest with an extremely ugly baby. Would you say, 'Ma'am, that is one extremely ugly baby?'"

"No, of course not!" he replied.

"Why not?"

"Because it would be rude!"

And that enabled me to explain that it was not dishonest to refrain from saying all that he knew. Just as it would be rude to tell the guest that her baby was ugly, it was also rude to burden the guest with information about his work schedule, home life, hobbies, and other personal details.

We need to avoid giving too much information, or acting as if the guest is a friend, a neighbor, or even someone we met at a party. Instead, we need to maintain the artificial barrier of server and guest. We need to respect the guest's privacy by not forcing our information, thoughts, or views onto them.

As a counter-example – again, like any aspect of customer service, or life in general, balance is everything – there is a coffee bar that I frequent on weekends. One of the shift leads calls me by my first name, and I call her by hers. She has offered me home-made baked goods from time to time. We sometimes exchange minor medical advice, such as "If that ankle doesn't get better by tomorrow, you really ought to go have it checked out."

Why is it okay for this young woman to be so friendly with me, and yet wrong for the maintenance man to be too friendly with hotel guests? Well, the key is the relationship. It's the difference between hugging an old classmate from high school and hugging a random stranger on the bus. One will get you a slap on the back, and the other will get you a slap on the face and most likely a restraining order.

If I were to walk into the coffee bar, having never been there before, and if the young woman were to offer me a home-baked churro from a batch she brought for her coworkers, that act would be grossly inappropriate. It is only because of the long time that we have known each other that we are able to be more familiar.

Even so, it would be inappropriate for me to ask her out, or for her to ask me out. Our casual barista-customer relationship, friendly as it is, still does not allow that level of familiarity.

Okay, I've probably confused you by giving you examples and counter-examples. I'll admit, the perfect balance of friendliness and distance is not always easy to achieve, and it's a bit of a judgement call. So let's look at some concrete steps you can take to help find that balance.

First, always smile. A friendly smile should suggest that you are approachable. It should not look like your teeth hurt, or like you have gas. If that is the effect that you're projecting, you might want to practice in a mirror until you get it right.

Next, keep your speech professional. "Enjoy the rest of your night" is always a good response, whereas "Hang loose" or "Take it easy" might convey a bit too much of a casual approach. Use polite words and phrases, like we talked about in the first chapter. On the one hand, don't be rude, and on the other hand, don't be too casual, and never ever flirt.

Finally, be ready to decline politely if a guest suggests that you meet somewhere later, or that you give him your phone number. In general, you should not accept anything from a guest that you would not accept from a random stranger on a bus.

In waiting on the table, the balance lies in listening to the guests, letting them express themselves, and then responding casually and calmly.

Casually greet the table and welcome the customers to the restaurant. Answer any questions that they may have: about the specials, how late you'll be open, or the locations of the restrooms, perhaps. Ask if they'd like drinks while they're reading the menu.

Do not remark on what hotties they are. Don't try out your best pickup line. Don't ask what brings them to your restaurant (obviously, it's the fact that they're hungry). Don't say how adorable the baby looks, or ask how old the preschooler may be. Don't tell them about the funny thing that happened on your way to work, or your dream of being a rock musician or an actor.

Let them ask questions, and be careful not to cut them off or to interrupt them. If the answer to a question is yes — can they get ranch dressing? — answer with a smile and a clear "Yes" or a "Certainly." If the answer is no — can they substitute onion rings for the cole slaw? — tell them that you are sorry, but no, that's not allowed. And if you are not certain of the answer (Is the Apfelstrudel gluten-free?) say that you aren't sure, and that you'll ask on their behalf.

Make sure that you carry through on the promise.

Notice, in all of these small interactions, that you are placing yourself on their side. You are their ambassador, their advocate, their link to the restaurant. You'll do whatever it takes to make their experience a happy one, within what the restaurant offers.

At the same time, you're separate and distinct from them. *We* (the restaurant) can certainly put ranch dressing on the salad; I'm sorry, but *we* (the restaurant) can't substitute onion rings for the cole slaw; I'm not sure, but I'll find out if *our* (the restaurant's) apfelstrudel is gluten-free.

The distance lies in the fact that you are part of the restaurant; the friendliness lies in being the tour guide for the guests. You stand in both worlds, and make the guests' interaction with the restaurant more enjoyable for them and more productive for the restaurant.

Find the balance, and use that balance. Friendly, but not familiar.

An important part of appropriate attention lies in recognizing the progress of the meal. A meal has several stages.

First, the guest is seated. A guest who is recently seated will be looking at the menu. The napkin probably will still be on the table, in the napkin ring or folded under the knife and fork. It might be on the guest's lap. The knife and fork will be on the table, to the guest's right. When you see that a table in your zone has just been seated, that is your cue to approach the table and to take drink orders.

Remember to stand in the guest's field of vision and wait to be seen. Then ask if there are any questions, and if you can take drink orders. Many restaurants place coasters in front of guests so that other servers will know that drink orders have been taken.

Next, the guest orders. A guest is ready to order when the menu has been set aside. The guest might be sipping her drink, staring at his cell phone, or conversing with the others at the table. Napkins should be in laps (might still be folded on the table), and utensils should still be on the tabletop, in parallel.

This is your cue to take orders. Casually approach the table. Wait to be noticed – don't just start speaking. Answer questions and take the order. Remember that accuracy is an important key to this step. Speak clearly, and if you don't understand an order, apologize and ask the guest to repeat.

One of my friends has trouble ordering coffee in a coffee bar, because he asks for whipped cream. His very slight accent and his soft voice cause it to sound like he has said "Wip cream" which baristas almost always interpret as "With [room for] cream." He has begun to say, "Add whipped," which seems to better get the idea across.

Be careful to listen to the order.

When you have taken the order, also take the menus. This gives the visual cue that the guests have ordered and are waiting for food. Keep an eye on the table, and remember that guests who wait too long may simply give up and walk out. If there is a delay – an error, a backlog in the kitchen, a shortage of scallions – come back to the table and let the guests know that it will be a while longer. And you're very sorry about that.

Be careful not to use restaurant jargon. One server remarked to a friend and me that the kitchen had just dropped our orders. She meant that the kitchen staff had just then begun to cook our food, that is, to "drop" it into the pan. My dinner companion misunderstood this to mean that the kitchen staff had prepared our food, but it had fallen onto the floor, and the order had to be thrown away and re-started.

This is the point at which your role as advocate for the guest comes into play. You need to be the translator: Speak kitchen jargon to help the kitchen staff understand what the guest wants, and speak in common civil terms to the guest. "The kitchen has just started on your order" would have been the better way to tell us the status of our meal.

Jargon is everywhere, and not just in customer service. I had something like this happen once, outside a professional setting, fortunately, with a law student who kept telling people that the information that they needed was "Stated supra." I had to break in and say that "Stated supra" meant "As it says up there." This was very helpful to the confused listener, though it made the law student angry. He then lectured me on the importance of using proper blue-book form (that's the standard format that lawyers use when writing papers and briefs).

Between us, I think he'd lost the plot, but it illustrates my point on jargon. He had no clue that, although he was speaking in the technically correct way for his industry, his listeners had no clue what he meant.

You need to have the same awareness of jargon that our law student friend clearly lacked. As the guests' connection to the restaurant, you must help the guests to understand, in common civil terms, what's happening in the kitchen while being the mouthpiece for the restaurant. You can say that you're sorry, but there's a slight delay because *we* need to prepare more scallions. You do not say that prep failed because there wasn't enough garnish to drop the order – those are jargon terms, understood in the kitchen but not in the dining room.

Through it all, you must keep the diners informed of what's happening in the kitchen. You must also keep an eye on the kitchen to see if the order is in progress. You never want food to "die in the window." That's the kitchen jargon for food that makes it to the serving window and gets cold waiting for you to pick it up.

The next stage begins when the food is served, and it should ideally be served to all guests at the same time. If this is not possible for some reason, do not forget the guests who have yet to be served. Apologize, let them know that the order is coming, and then keep an eye on the window so that you can serve them promptly.

I once sat in a restaurant watching my friends finish their meal. The server was nowhere around. Finally, well into the meal, the server reappeared and casually asked, "Can I get anyone anything else?"

I replied, "Well, I'd like my order, please." She was utterly shocked that, despite having ordered with everyone else, I still did not have my food. To this day, we refer to that event as the three-hour lunch.

The waiter was not attentive. Granted, she also avoided being intrusive, and once she realized the mistake, she corrected it as quickly as she could. However, she should have been aware of the omission before I was. She should have had her eye on the table from time to time.

Within five minutes of the food being served – especially if one of the other servers helped you out by delivering the food – stop at the table and ask if everything is to the guests' liking. Scan for missing orders. Look at glasses, to see if refills are in order.

Remember, as always, to step into the field of vision and then wait to be noticed. If you must interrupt a guest who is speaking, say, "Pardon me; I'm sorry to interrupt." Then proceed to ask if everything is alright.

At this stage of the meal, the guests are eating, utensils are in use, and napkins are on laps. If a guest gets up from the table and intends to return, he will place the napkin on his chair and lay the utensils on the table beside his plate. A glass or cup placed at the edge of the table is intended to be refilled.

If a guest leaves the table and isn't returning, the napkin will be on the table, and the utensils will be on the plate, in parallel. The napkin may even be on the plate.

If the guests are sitting at the table with the utensils in parallel on the plate, and the napkin on the table or on the plate, you can be confident that the guests are finished with the meal (or with that course, at least). This is the time to approach the table, ask if the guests would like to see a desert menu, and to ask if their plates can be removed.

Once the plates are removed, if the guests are ordering dessert, then the process returns to the ordering stage. Otherwise, it's time to bring the check. The check should be placed face down on the table or on a small tray of some sort. If the customer has not expressly asked for the check, it is courteous to say, "There's no hurry, but this is here when you're ready for it." You might also ask, before delivering the check, "Are you ready for the check?"

Some restaurants may make it a policy not to bring the check until it is expressly asked for. In that case, you will want to keep an eye on the table so that you will see the raised hand, or the guest's nod. Always follow the process and procedures that your manager has given you.

When the check has been delivered, keep an eye on it. You should see payment appear soon thereafter. Pick up the check and the payment promptly. If the guest is paying by card, process the transaction promptly as well. Make sure to return the card when you deliver the processed slip.

The payment process, from the business perspective, is the most important part. Once you leave the check on the table, it would be a bad moment to go into the kitchen to do your side work, or to check the vacation schedule. Good customer service continues up until the moment that the guest walks out the door.

With the card returned, your job is almost done. All that remains is for the guest to sign the slip and to total it with any tip that she may wish to leave. You should still check on the table from time to time, especially if the guests sit and chat for a while.

This is probably as good a place as any to talk about tips. Tips are also called gratuities, from the Latin word *gratis,* meaning "free." It is a gift that is freely given at the pleasure of the guest. You are not owed a tip. You did not earn a tip. The customer does not have to give a tip.

It's a good practice to tip, and I, personally, try to tip well whenever I can. It helps the server, it expresses my gratitude, and it tends to make me more welcome when I return. But it is not necessary to tip, and the guests are not at all obligated to do so.

Yes, you may be paid a low wage on the assumption that the wages will be offset by tips. That is not the guest's problem. It still does not entitle you to a tip simply because you happened to be responsible for that particular table. And if you keep that in mind, on average, tips will work out well for you.

In Europe, tipping is not generally done, or the tip is very tiny. This varies by country, of course, but in most European countries, the coins from your change will suffice. In other countries, such as England, a tip of about 10% is normal. In Japan, a tip is regarded as almost an insult.

The 15%, and sometimes 20%, that some guests in the United States choose freely to give to servers who serve well, is very generous. It must not be taken for granted.

If a guest does not tip, ignore this oversight. I know of a hotel where a server followed a European guest from the café and stopped him in the lobby to ask, "Was there something wrong with the service?"

It turned out that the man had left a very small tip – just coins, as is common in Europe. The server was severely reprimanded for her actions. Asking for a tip or complaining about a tip are never appropriate actions, and in some places, can result in termination. If a guest tips well, think well of that guest and spend the money joyfully. If a guest does not tip well, look for areas where you can improve your service, and try to think well of that guest anyway.

Don't misunderstand me. My sympathy is with the server. I do hold wait staff to a high standard, and I do expect professionalism regardless of the situation. I also know that this coin has two sides.

One afternoon, a family I know invited me to join them at a local restaurant for a late lunch. Due to circumstances beyond my control, I arrived about twenty minutes after they had begun eating. They had saved me a seat, but it was difficult to flag down a waiter for a menu, and difficult to place the order once I was ready.

In the course of conversation, it came up that the family had been very demanding (they would say that they had merely asked for reasonable things, like a large number of substitutions and modifications), and that the wait staff had (rightly, in my opinion) taken umbrage at their behavior.

If that family should read this – I'm sorry, but the lot of you were exceptionally rude to the waiters.

As we prepared to leave, I folded together a small cash tip and left it under the edge of my plate. A grown daughter of the family, sitting to my right, picked up the tip and stuffed it into my shirt pocket, saying, "Don't leave a tip! The service was horrible!"

I removed the tip from my pocket and put it back under the plate. "Yes," I said, "But I might want to eat here when you haven't already exasperated the staff."

When you are the guest, please keep in mind that waiting tables is seldom a job one chooses just because it seems like fun. In one hotel, I knew a room service attendant who literally lived on his tips. His wages were almost entirely garnished, due to some poor decisions and some drama in his personal life, so only his tips were available for paying the rent and putting food on the table.

Tips can be that important. Had he been in a non-tipping job, he would have starved, and his family would have suffered.

Nonetheless, when you are the waiter, always take the high road. If someone doesn't tip, ignore it. Assume that they didn't know the custom, or that they were short on cash, or simply forgot.

Over all, if you perform good service, you will generally see good tips, on average. If you are not seeing good tips, ask yourself if you are providing good service. To improve your tips, improve your service. Be attentive without being intrusive, and be friendly without being familiar.

Chapter Three:
The Customer is NOT Always Right.

IT USED TO BE a rule of thumb that the customer is always right. The large department store, Nordstrom's, allegedly used to have a customer service training video that showed a customer returning snow tires without a receipt. The key to remember is that Nordstrom's doesn't sell snow tires.

A certain major hotel chain used a customer service slogan in its training one year, "Never Say No." If I want my room for free, does "Never Say No" mean that I don't have to pay?

Endless hours have been spent teaching hospitality staff to feel "empowered" about helping guests to resolve issues. The takeaway that is pounded into these training sessions is that everything possible must be done to give guests whatever they want. After all, the important question is whether the guest will return another time, right?

While well-intentioned, this training misses an important factor: Guests are not always reasonable. As with anything in life, balance is the key to customer service. If you spill coffee on a guest's shirt, it is reasonable to pick up his tab for lunch and to offer to have the shirt dry-cleaned. It is not reasonable to offer him free coffee for life. It is not reasonable to offer to reverse all charges for a week-long hotel stay.

The make-good needs to be in the same scope and scale as the issue that makes it necessary. If a meal is ruined, a free meal is a reasonable remedy. If a night's stay in the hotel is ruined – for example, if the bed breaks, or the breaker keeps blowing out – then a night's stay (which might be a discount on that night's stay, or a future discount for another stay) would be reasonable.

A very extreme example occurred one evening when I had Manager on Duty responsibility at a certain hotel. There was a popular event that weekend, and almost every hotel room in town was sold out. We had one room left to sell, with a two-night minimum, and it was almost certain to sell within the next hour.

I was on my way home for the evening when the front desk clerk called me back. I arrived to find a family of four sitting in the lobby. The man was standing at the front desk.

The desk clerk informed me that the man had no reservation, but believed he had been promised the room at half price. To try to make things right, the clerk had offered him the last room we had, at a discount, and was willing to release the two-night minimum, but he didn't want it. Also, he didn't want that particular room, even though it was the last room we had.

After hearing from the clerk what the man had been offered, I asked the man how I could help him. He insisted that he had called for reservations – he didn't know the name of the agent to whom he had spoken – and that he had been told that the nightly rate was for two nights. Relying on that alleged promise, he had released a reservation at another hotel and had come straight here for that rate on that room.

You will understand, of course, that there are two major problems with this:

First, he did actually not have a reservation. He had spoken to a reservations agent, but a reservation is not complete until it is confirmed. That is the point where the reservationist reads back all of the details to you and then has you confirm that you are reserving X number of room-nights at Y rate. The reservationist then gives you a reservations number.

This man had no reservation. He had hung up on the reservationist in order to rush down to our hotel and grab that room. He had no reservation number, and could not even name the reservationist who had allegedly offered him this deal.

The second problem is that, at the very least, he had misunderstood the reservationist. The reservationist, in telling him that the reservation was for two nights, meant that he would need to pay the specified amount twice – once for each night, for the two night minimum. He had assumed (I'm being generous; I think he probably knew what he was doing) that the rate was for both nights, combined, thus each night would be half that.

If I were following the Never-Say-No mentality, I might have offered him a half-price room, just because he had misunderstood what the reservationist meant. And I would have been answerable to the General Manager for the loss of revenue.

If I were following the Nordstrom's mentality, I would have given him the room at half-price and thrown in a discount for next year's stay. But in this case, the customer was not right.

There was a third problem as well. The room we offered – our last room – was a smaller room (still a large room, you understand) and was adjacent to the lobby. Those two conditions were unacceptable to him. If he had listened to the reservationist, and heard all of the details before canceling his old reservation, he would have heard these facts.

But instead, he was livid that we were offering him a room that was unacceptable to him, at a price that was unacceptable to him. How dare we?

When I asked him what he wanted me to do, he said that he wanted a different room (and he was still rigidly demanding the half-priced rate). I raised an eyebrow.

"So what you're telling me, Sir," I calmly asked, "Is that you'd like me to wake up another guest, have that guest pack up and move down here, and then give you that guest's room? You know that I can't do that."

Notice here that I was restating what the guest was asking. I was still telling him the truth: I can't reasonably inconvenience another guest just to give him his preferred room. Had the hotel not been sold out – and had the guest not been so stubborn – I might have rearranged the existing room list, looking for any guests who hadn't yet checked in, in order to give him a different room.

But I was offering him a very nice room, more than adequate for his purposes, at a discounted rate. Still, he wasn't budging an ounce. We had to have another room available (clearly, we were all lying to him, you see) and he had been promised a half-price rate. He was certain of these things (he claimed), and he would have them though the heavens fall!

I don't recommend being aggressive with customers. If this sort of thing ever happens to you, just call your manager immediately. Let the manager be the bad guy. In this case, I was the manager, so I had to be the bad guy. So I raised the ante on him.

"Well, Sir," I said, "We have two choices. You can accept this room for one night at the discounted rate, or, I'm willing to release you from the cancellation fee, and you can go to another hotel."

Here's the thing: He didn't have a reservation so there wouldn't have been a cancellation fee. But if he said that he didn't owe a cancellation fee, he would be admitting that he didn't have a reservation. And if he demanded that he had a reservation, then he would be liable for a cancellation fee.

"A cancellation fee?"

"Well, yes, Sir," I politely explained. "Normally, for a reservation cancelled within 24 hours of arrival, I would have to charge one night's room rate and taxes. But since you don't like the room, and since I'm sure that I can re-sell the room, I'll gladly waive the fee."

We went back and forth – I had to restate the offer a couple of times, each time resisting the urge to simply tell him to get out of my lobby. Remember, good customer service is all about self-control.

Finally, the third time that I offered him the room at the discounted rate, his wife piped up and said, "Why do you always do this? Just take the room!" And thus cooler heads prevailed.

Now, was this proper customer service?

You might be saying that it wasn't. After all, I didn't give the guest what he wanted. I didn't leave him happy when he walked away. He may have never stayed with us again.

And I've just finished telling you that those are all cardinal sins of customer service.

But let's consider it carefully. First, I answered politely each time. I used "Sir" when I spoke to him. I was not rude. I was firm, but I was not rude. I did not use bad language, and I did not yell.

Secondly, I offered him what we had available. We offered him the best possible rate per our guidelines. And we waived the two-night minimum. Those were both large concessions on our part. Many hotels would not have done that.

Third, I made the choice obvious and binary. We would graciously release him from his reservation, or he could take the room that we were offering at the rate we were offering.

I did not offer him any surprises. I didn't change what we were offering. I didn't disappear in the middle of the discussion. I was prompt and attentive. I was not familiar, nor was I unfriendly.

Just as you can be truthful without saying everything you know, you can also be polite and still be firm. You can provide excellent customer service without giving away the hotel.

How do you know the difference between being rude and inflexible, or being polite but firm? Well, ask yourself a few questions:

1. Are you being friendly in tone and polite in your speech?
2. Is what you're offering reasonable? Is the product you're selling worth the price you're asking?
3. Is the remedy you're offering the right size for the issue that you're correcting?
4. Would you be satisfied with the remedy that you are offering?

You will need to know the policies and approved procedures for your workplace before taking any action regarding remedies for guest issues. Your company should have customer service standards, including appropriate remedies, and should explain them clearly. If you should find yourself in a situation that you're not prepared to handle, do as the front desk agent did, and call your manager.

Another example of the customer not being right falls into the category of outright fraud. A certain front desk clerk was working when a customer came in and asked to have ten ten-dollar bills converted to a one-hundred dollar bill. This is actually a good transaction when it happens, because it helps the front desk to be able to make change for other cash-paying customers.

While she was getting the hundred dollar bill, the customer picked up the ten tens and "counted" them again before putting them back on the counter. The problem is that the customer took back three of the bills. Then the customer asked for two or three other rapid transactions, all designed around keeping the front desk clerk from realizing that she was being short-changed. In the end, the customer walked away with about one-hundred dollars too much, and the front desk clerk had to make up the shortfall. It wasn't until the security video was replayed that it became obvious what had happened.

There are several safeguards to observe when handling money. One of these is that you never let the customer touch money that they have given to you. When a customer hands you money, accept it from him, thank him, and then place it out of his reach. Make change, and give the customer change. If the customer starts handing bills back to you, stop him. State that you can only do one transaction at a time.

Complete giving him the change. Then, and only then, put away the original bill. And then, if he wishes additional transactions, you may perform those transactions.

Remember that not every guest is honest, and not every request is sincere. A customer who is trying to steal from you is not right, and you need not honor the request. You can be friendly, but firm. It is possible to say nearly anything politely, with practice, including, "I'm sorry Sir, but I'm going to have to call the police."

It is a digression from the point of this chapter, but this might be a good time to talk about how to give someone money. It is a common practice to give someone change by putting bills on their hand, then the receipt, and then the coins like a paperweight. Please never, ever, do this.

The customer will not be able to put that mess into her pocket. She's going to spill coins everywhere trying to grasp it. Coins will roll all over the counter, onto the floor. The customer will not be happy, and neither will you.

Instead, do this: Place the coins into the hollow of the customer's palm. Then place the bills on top. Let the customer close her thumb on the bills. Then ask the customer if she wants a receipt. This way, the customer can put the bills and coins into a pocket without spilling anything, and the receipt – usually the least flexible paper of all – can be accepted, if she desires it, after the money is put away.

Yes, you're in a hurry to hand off the receipt efficiently. But the customer's convenience takes precedence over your efficiency. Yes, it seems natural to put the coins on top, because they are the smallest and because it seems like they'd serve as a paperweight. But since there's probably not a hurricane in your lobby, just don't do it.

Next, at the risk of offending all the managers and business owners out there, I should also tell you that sometimes the rules themselves are not right.

One afternoon, a friend and I had just stopped for coffee when we realized that we were near the local bowling alley. We wanted to get pricing for games and shoe rentals, since we were planning a group outing within the next month. To be fair, we should have finished our coffee before walking in, but we did not.

There were conspicuous signs telling us that outside food and drink were not allowed. But since we would only be inside for a moment, we went inside anyway.

As we waited to speak to the clerk at the bowling counter, a food service person came over to us. He may have been the food service manager; I'm not certain.

"Hey," he said. "You can't bring that in here."

"Yeah, sorry," I started to say. "We just wanted to check – "

"You need to leave right now."

"Right, we're going, we –"

"You can't have that in here, you need to leave."

"Okay, – "

"YOU NEED TO LEAVE, NOW!"

Okay, he was right. He was absolutely in the right. It was the rule, I was in violation of the rule, and I should have known and followed the rule. But what was the intention of the rule?

A rule that says, "No outside food or drink is allowed" is intended to preserve the bowling alley's monopoly on food eaten in the bowling alley. If I had been there to bowl, or to eat, or to do any of the other amusements offered by the bowling alley, it would have been very appropriate to politely tell me that outside food was not allowed, and to eject me if I didn't comply.

The gentleman chose to follow the rule even when the rule made no sense in my case. Under no circumstances was I going to purchase anything during that visit. Thus, the bowling alley did not suffer financially from the fact that I was holding a cup of coffee.

He also chose to be very rude about it. Both of these are simply poor choices.

Suppose that the conversation had gone like this:

"Excuse me, Sir, but outside food is not allowed."

"Sorry. I'm just here to get some information about pricing. I'll be gone in five minutes."

"Okay, but in the future, please be aware of the rule. Thank you for your cooperation."

If the conversation had gone like that, I probably would not remember the incident, or I would remember it sheepishly. If I ever told anyone about it, the point would be how polite the fellow had been, while firmly reminding me that I had made a mistake.

Instead, this experience will always stand out to me as a glaring example of poor customer service. Don't get me wrong; I wasn't angry over it, and I certainly did go back to that bowling alley after that. In fact, several friends and I later rented a couple of lanes and made a pleasant afternoon out of it. But I like to think that I am more patient than the average customer off the street. Most folks would not have been so gracious.

If you find yourself in this sort of situation, please do what this gentleman did not do: Ask yourself the purpose of the rule, and if it applied in this situation. Since I would not have been consuming any food or drink inside the bowling alley, chastising me for holding a paper cup of coffee was not appropriate.

Next, even if the rule does apply, be polite. I suggested a politer alternative above, and here are some others that could be used in this sort of situation:

"Hi, just so that you know, we don't allow any outside food or drink." Or, "Excuse me, but would you mind taking that outside? We don't allow outside food." Possibly even, "Hi, and thanks for being our guest today, but our policy is that you can't have that in here." Those alternatives are much nicer, and consistent with both the rule and with proper customer service.

As we were saying, the customer is not always right, just as I wasn't right in the case of this bowling alley caper. Even when the customer is not right, follow good customer service guidelines. If necessary, be gentle, but firm.

As we have seen, the customer is often not right.

The customer may be trying to take advantage of you, or the customer may be asking for something unreasonable. In any case, be polite but firm. Follow (and understand) the policies of your workplace. Make sure that remedies are appropriate to the issue that made them necessary. When in doubt, ask your manager for guidance.

Remain friendly and polite. But don't "Give away the hotel."

Chapter Four:
This Ain't No Disco.
(This chapter features LIVE MUSIC!)

      LONG AGO, ONBOARD A certain US Navy ship that will remain nameless, there was a Mess Specialist Senior Chief who was famous for the remark, "This ain't no disco!"

He would say this when he saw people standing around on the mess decks, idly leaning against the coffee machine and chatting among themselves. He wanted these folks to move along, and not to hang out like they would at a disco or social club.

That fact – that this ain't no disco – is something that we should all remember. The business exists to serve customers and hopefully to make money while doing so. The byproduct of doing business is that we all have jobs, and make money ourselves.

The workplace is not our personal lounge. We don't come here to converse among ourselves, listen to music, and hang around. We're here to do a job.

When you walk into the lobby, you should be there for a purpose. Do that purpose and leave. Don't lean against the front counter and chat up the front desk clerk. Don't use the front desk phone to call your partner and tell him that you'll be late. So far as your behavior shows, the customer should be able to believe that you exist for the sole purpose of providing excellent customer service.

There's nothing wrong with chatting while you're on break, in the break room, out of sight and sound of the guests. There's nothing wrong with calling home, provided it's permitted by your business, and you use a phone located where none of the customers can see you or hear you.

Suppose that you walked into a restaurant, and the server was busy chatting with the bartender. Is that what you would expect to see, or would you rather be seated at a table and given menus?

Suppose that you walked into a hotel, and the front desk clerk was on a lengthy phone conversation telling her partner that the dog was overdue for a visit to the vet. Wouldn't you prefer that the clerk's attention was directed towards you, and that you were expeditiously checked in and shown to your room?

If your behavior isn't the behavior you would want to see, as a guest of the hotel, or customer of the restaurant, then don't do it. Don't treat the business as your private party place.

This includes maintaining a reasonable sound level, both in your conversations with other staff, and in the sound system, if any. Many hotels will have soft music playing in the lobby as an enhancement to the environment. Many restaurants will keep some sort of soft music playing while the guests are eating. But the sound system is NOT your personal stereo system.

Do not, and I will repeat, do not, turn the music up to eleven and rock out to it as you work. Even if it's your favorite song, and you can only hear the guitar riffs right when it's really, really, loud – Don't do it. Just don't do it.

Music for restaurants and hotels is meant to be not-silence. It's just meant to be a mild sound in the background, almost unnoticed, so that there is not utter silence. Silence is actually better than too much music.

Why are your guests sitting in the restaurant? Is it so that they can hear the wild sounds of that one really intense party song you love? No. They are there to eat, and possibly to talk among themselves. They won't be able to talk among themselves if your volume is off the scale.

But wait, you may say. There was a magazine article, and a YouTube video, and a TV show where this one expert said that making the restaurant slightly uncomfortable will encourage people to leave. Then you can turn the tables faster and serve more covers in an evening.

The problem with that advice – assuming that it's even an actual strategy, and not some TV producer's idea – is that the customers may not come back. If you ever want to make sure that I don't visit your restaurant more than once, have loud music blaring from the speakers. I guarantee that if I have to shout to be understood across the table, or, worse, have to shout to make my order clear to the server, I will not be back. Ever.

I did make an exception for one place, and that is because, on arriving, I immediately asked the server if the music could be turned down. The server did it at once. I left a good tip. And I wrote to the manager, to compliment the server.

To make certain that I don't visit your restaurant even once, simply put out one small sign with the words LIVE MUSIC on it. You will never see me in that place. Not once.

There are places where live music is appropriate. For example, in a very nice white-tablecloth establishment, some gentle piano music at a background level is nice. In a bar, on Cinco de Mayo, bring on the Mariachi band with unmuted trumpets. In a roadhouse or a "honky-tonk," by all means, play the music loud. For dancing, go full on and bring an orchestra if the mood strikes you. If there's a real honest-to-goodness mosh-pit in your business, crank the amps till your ears bleed (within the permissible sound levels approved by OSHA standards, of course).

But in a restaurant that is none of these, skip it. Loud music does nothing to improve or enhance the eating experience. But wait, you say. We don't have to play the music loud. Surely a few oldie-moldy tunes on an electric guitar will bring people back to their youth, and encourage them to have a good time.

Unfortunately, with amplified music, there is a fine line between not enough and way over the top. If your restaurant is smaller than 10,000 square feet, and you must have music, go with acoustic instruments only, and no brass. If it's smaller than 5,000 square feet, take away the singer's microphone. If it's smaller than 2,000 square feet, don't bother. Just don't do it at all.

Remember that music will reverberate off of the walls and echo, out of sync with the original source. If you have any doubts, walk into your restaurant while it's closed and clap your hands.

Hear that spiky echo that comes back from the corners? That's a killer when it comes to music. If your customers want to talk, they will resent loud interfering noise echoing from the corners. If they are unfortunate enough to have poor hearing, or to use hearing aids, you'll drive them mad.

It's bad enough when that one really drunk customer, who can't laugh without shrieking, cuts loose and damages the ear drums of everyone in the room. It's even worse when your over-amped singer hits a high note able to shatter wineglasses in the restaurant next door.

I'll make an exception to the no-live-music rule. I was at an event in a small local bookstore – a Jolabokaflodid celebration, if I recall – and the music was entirely appropriate. The musician set her amps to a reasonable level, and she could be clearly heard throughout the store, but it wasn't over the top and didn't keep us from talking among ourselves, nor did it keep the book monger from selling books. It was perfect.

If your musician is so astute – I believe that in this case, she sang under the name Kazuvius – that she can tune her amp for the size of the room, and be heard without drowning out all other sound, then you've found a rare pearl. Pay her well and make sure that customers tip. But it is so rare for a musician to be that self-aware that it is almost unheard of. This is a case where the exception makes the rule: When it comes to live music in small spaces, don't do it.

On another topic: when the Senior Chief said those memorable words, cell phones weren't yet a thing. The general public had no idea that any such thing was even possible. But if cell phones had been around, I'm fairly sure that I know what Senior would have said about them.

No one should ever see you on your cell phone. If you are in the public view, your cell phone should be in your pocket, or better yet, in your locker, in the basement of the hotel.

You may be using your cell phone to alert a guest to a change in their reservation; you may be looking up places nearby where the guest can get authentic Winnipeg-style pierogis. However, to the casual passerby, it looks like you're playing a video game, or checking your social media status. That status will be "Fired," if you don't put that phone away!

Using a cell phone, when it is obvious that you are an employee of the business, says to the customer that talking to your friends and playing video games is more important than doing your job.

In any case, as a hospitality professional, do not hang around where the customers can see and hear you. Do not play the music for your own entertainment. Do not use your cell phone during business hours. Keep in mind the reason and purpose for being at work.

Above all, just remember: This ain't no disco.

**Chapter Five:
When it all goes badly: The ARES method.**

THERE ARE GOING TO be angry customers. Sooner or later, you will be confronted by someone who is not having a good day. There will be tears. There will be shouting. There will be sound and fury, with lightning and thunder.

I have a method for dealing with these situations. I call it ARES, for Attitude, Reaction, Expectations, and Solutions.

Don't get excited. Don't lose your head. The first and most important thing is that you do not mirror what you see in front of you. If someone is angry with you, the natural tendency is to get angry back. But if you can remain calm, you will send them a subtle signal to calm down themselves. It costs you nothing to remain calm and to remain polite. It's all about ATTITUDES.

The second most important thing is to realize that the customer is not angry with you. The customer is angry about the circumstances; you merely happen to be standing in front of him or her. Don't take it personally. It's not about you. It's a REACTION.

Once you've controlled your reaction, and understood that their reaction is not a reflection on you, the next step is to find out what's wrong. What was the customer expecting, and what did the customer receive? Those are the EXPECTATIONS.

For example, maybe the customer ordered a cheeseburger with no mayonnaise, and received a mayo burger with no cheese. Maybe the customer asked for no broccoli, and got double broccoli. Maybe the customer booked a double double room, and got a queen room.

The final step is to offer options to make it right. SOLUTIONS.

Remember the guy who wanted a half-price room during a sold-out weekend when we had one room left to sell – but did NOT want the last room we had?

First, I remained calm. The customer was angry, but I was not. I did not mirror his emotions. I realized that his anger was not about me. I controlled my Attitude, despite his.

I did not React in the same way that he was reacting. Instead, I maintained my professional calm.

Next, I found out what he Expected – a room for one night at half price, when the rate was for a two-night minimum; and a room that was not the one offered.

Then I offered him options for a Solution or a remedy. We would let him have the room for the one night only, at the discounted rate (but not half price) or we would release him from the cancellation and allow him to go elsewhere. Attitudes, Reaction, Expectations, Solutions. You could make an acronym from that: ARES.

We will use the ARES method as we examine what to do about angry or unhappy guests.

Suppose that a customer is screaming that there is no lemon in her tea. Or too much lemon flavor. Or both.

Let's apply the ARES method.

> ATTITUDE: Speak calmly and professionally at all times. Be attentive, but don't mirror her attitude.
> REACTION: Realize that it's not about you; don't react.
> EXPECTATION: Calmly ask what she had ordered, so that you will know what she expects.
> SOLUTIONS: Offer her a choice, to remake the drink, or to bring something else that might be more to her liking.

So far so good. Let's try some other scenarios. Suppose that a waiter trips and spills tomato soup all over a table of diners. How might we apply ARES?

> ATTITUDE: Be apologetic, but do not mirror the anger you see in front of you.
> REACTION: React calmly, but apologetically. You're terribly sorry.
> EXPECTATION: The guests most likely expected not to be splattered with soup. I'm just guessing here...
> SOLUTION: Following the guidelines for your workplace, offer two or more options for solutions. Depending on the guidelines, you might offer to pay for their meal, or to have the clothes dry cleaned.

We need to say a bit more about solutions. As we discussed in chapter 3 ("The Customer Is Not Always Right"), the solution needs to be proportionate to the issue. A meal for a meal; a night's stay for a night's stay; a free movie pass for a ruined movie outing.

If you ruin a guest's shirt with tomato soup, chances are that they won't want a 10% off coupon for their next meal (not unless it was a very expensive meal and a very cheap shirt). If your valet parking staff accidentally set fire to a guest's car, a free meal might not be enough to make things right.

On the other hand, mispronouncing a guest's name should not earn him a free room night. That the guest waited twenty-five minutes for an omelet should not entitle her to a free meal. In either or those cases, a coupon or a small reduction in the bill might be appropriate.

The exact guideline for what is appropriate and what is NOT appropriate will be a matter for your manager to decide. When in doubt, consult your shift lead, manager, or other authority.

There is another point to address when we speak of angry guests, and that is that you must always be apologetic towards the guest's experience without ever apologizing for the event itself. For example, suppose that a guest trips while walking to the front desk, and falls on the floor. You would definitely want to help him, and you want to be apologetic. But consider the difference between these two statements:

1. I'm terribly sorry that this happened to you, Sir. Do you think that you might need medical attention? Should I call for a doctor?

2. I'm terribly sorry about that, Sir. That floor is very slick, especially when it's wet. Someone probably spilled something. We'll get that cleaned up right away.

The difference — and again, you will want to strictly follow your workplace policies — the difference is that the second statement admits liability. In the second statement, you've implied that it is the hotel's fault that the guest fell down, and that the floor might have been wet.

This could lead to serious problems, especially if the guest staged the fall in order to have grounds to sue the hotel. Customers aren't always right, you know.

Better still would be simply to say, "Are you alright? Should I call for medical attention?" Then you are giving the guest options (Solutions) that do not imply that the hotel is at fault.

The worst possible thing would be to blame the hotel, or to tell the guest that the hotel would pay to fix the problem. This would be an admission of responsibility, whether you are right or wrong about the cause of the incident. Let the hotel managers take responsibility for determining what happened, and what should be done about it in the long term. Your job is to deal with the immediate problem.

Should a safety-related incident occur at your workplace, follow the policies established by your management, and inform your manager right away, so that the manager can take the appropriate steps.

This principle does not merely apply to safety-related incidents.

Once, while working as a telephone system service technician, I was sent to a customer's site because some of the mailboxes had been hacked. A caller had guessed the very weak passcodes on these mailboxes, and set them to notify his pager.

I quickly went through the system and changed the passcodes of the hacked mailboxes, removing the notifications and the odd custom messages that the hacker had created. I set stronger passcodes, and then went to the business owner, to have him sign off the work order.

The business owner demanded that I change the master passcode for the system, saying that my boss had said that the master mailbox had also been hacked. I saw no sign of this, and said so to the customer, but I did as the customer wished. He signed off the work order and I went back to the shop.

Later, the boss came to see me. The customer was saying that I had told him that the master mailbox had been hacked. For whatever reason, the customer was lying to me about what my boss said, and lying to my boss about what I said.

Imagine if I had said anything that even sounded like, "We'll take care of that for you" or "This is all my fault." This customer would have spun that into an international conspiracy, possibly involving Three Letter Agencies, Elvis, and a tie to Watergate.

Always be careful when something goes wrong. Do not even take on responsibility for an injury or other mishap. Let your manager sort out the proper remedy and response.

When a customer is angry or rude, follow the ARES method:

Attitude,
Reaction,
Expectation,
Solution.

Chapter 6
Retail Sales

THERE ARE TWO THINGS that never fail to annoy a retail customer, and they are the same two things that are the cardinal sins of table-waiting. The first is for the customer service representatives to vanish into thin air. The second is for them to hover over the customer and demand to help him.

There is an electronics shop in my town. It's a large retailer, with a name that you would recognize. They carry a dizzying array of fun and interesting electronics. But at least one of my friends will not go into the store, or will only enter when the products he wants are not available anywhere else, including online.

"You can't browse," he says. "You have to walk in with your head down, and move quickly past the 'Can I help you?' chorus at the front of the store. Then, when you get to a product that interests you, and that you might wish to buy, you can't read the specifications because clerks keep appearing and asking to help you with it." He will usually sigh at this point. "I want to know if it has the features I need, and if it's compatible with my other devices. Instead, I have to keep telling clerks, that, no, I'm fine, please leave me alone."

Remember the rules that we gave for waiting on tables. We want to be attentive but not intrusive. In retail, that means being aware of customers, and being approachable should they need us – that's the part about being attentive. We must also give the customer time to look at the products without us tugging on their sleeves for attention – that's the part about not being intrusive.

Imagine if you walked into a grocery store, and each time you stopped by a product, someone raced up and began to talk to you about the product. "Good morning, Ma'am! I see that you're looking at the chicken soup! Do you have any questions about it? Would you like me to see if we have vegetable beef in stock? Or beef stock in stock? Can I show you our lovely line of bisques and chowders? Have you seen our bouillabaisse?"

I shudder to imagine something like that.

Even worse than that, imagine if one certain soup brand were to have its own salesmen in the store, trying to push a monthly soup subscription onto all of the customers who walked in, even if they only came to buy, say, bread and luncheon meat. Do you think that many of those customers would return a second time?

Obviously, if that's too over-the-top in a grocery store, it's also too over-the-top in an electronics store, or a clothing store, or a home improvement store, or nearly any store at all. So why would we think that customers want to have us pounce on them and make them feel hunted?

Remember, your goal is to be an ambassador for the store to the customer, and an ambassador to the customer for the store. Your job is to make it easier for the customer to find and to buy what they want, and easy for the store to provide what the customer is asking for.

There may be times when you want to approach a customer. If a customer looks confused, or is looking up and down the aisles, then it might be acceptable to say, "Excuse me, but you seem puzzled. Is there anything I can help you find?"

If the customer says no, then let the customer be. You might still stay nearby. You definitely shouldn't take it as a personal rejection, and go hide in the alley behind the store. But do give the customer a chance to look at the merchandise and make a good decision.

In general, if the customer is looking at the products, reading the boxes, and comparing the items on the shelf, the customer is already doing your job for you. They are selling themselves on the features of the product. Don't interrupt them and break their chain of thought, but do be close by for questions that they may have.

If a customer has spent a long time in one place, you might approach once to ask if she has any questions. But only once. And no other sales person should approach that same customer.

Granted, there are customers who bear watching. A customer who is furtive, or who keeps looking around to see where the cameras and mirrors are – that customer might warrant a "How can I help you?" and a close eye. A bit of hovering might be in order, to make sure that merchandise isn't going into a pocket.

But in the general case, hovering is almost never good. Make customers feel welcome, but never hunted. Ask yourself, "Would this behavior in a salesperson make me feel uncomfortable, if I were the guest?"

With that, we must acknowledge that tastes in customer service vary. Some people want to have a massive entourage following them around. One man I knew became so impressed, by the fact that a shopkeeper was following him through the store, that he purchased an expensive tie, just to be polite. It turned out that the shopkeeper had mistaken him for a certain celebrity. I suppose that maybe there was a slight resemblance.

As in everything, balance is the key to success in retail customer service. We wish to be attentive, but not intrusive, and friendly, without being familiar.

If we may digress for a moment, to think about how the customer experience can become unbalanced, and can quickly overload the abilities of the sales staff, there is yet another story that we should consider.

In a certain coffee store chain, it is customary to have one person making drinks and one person at the register, taking orders. A third person may jump in at either station when needed, or may clean tables, stock shelves, and assist guests on the floor.

This particular day, the staff members were all relatively unfamiliar with the store and its stock. The reason for that is not important to the story. A customer looked over the shelves, trying to find a certain product, and when he couldn't see what he wanted, stopped the third sales person. The sales person went to the same shelves where the customer had looked, and started a new search.

When the sales person came to the same conclusion as the customer, she went to the person at the register and asked for help.

This led to three people searching for the product, and no one taking orders. The line stopped.

When none of them could find the product, they then stopped the person making the coffee, and soon the customer and three salespersons – the entire active store staff – were all searching in vain for a product that should have been, but was not, on that shelf. The line was out the door. No one was taking orders, and no one was making coffee for the orders already taken.

The manager came in just as the customers in line were starting to give up and walk out of the store. She managed to get things back on track, but it was too late: The damage had already been done.

What went wrong? Weren't these people providing great customer service? Weren't they going the extra mile to help find that product? Didn't that one customer receive great service?

Yes, it's true that they provided fantastic customer service to that one customer. But in doing so, they provided poor service to some of the customers (those who had ordered but didn't get their drinks timely), and no service at all to the customers who walked out the door.

What should they have done differently?

The first person who was unable to find the desired product should have stopped and said, "I'm sorry, but I'm new here and don't know where else we might have that. If I find it later, is there a number where I can reach you to let you know?"

Alternatively, the first sales person could have said, "If you're able to wait for a few minutes, I can ask my colleagues as soon as they're free."

The person taking orders, in turn, should have been able to say, "I'm sorry, but I have to take orders, and I can help you search once the line has stopped." The person making the drink orders should have been able to say something similar.

Alternatively, any of these could have found the manager and asked for further guidance or help. If anyone knows how the store is stocked, it should be the manager. Even if the manager were busy with something else, interrupting the manager is a better option than stopping all service to resolve a single question.

Do not allow a single issue or a single customer to take up the entire staff's attention. Know when to politely "put someone on hold," and always feel free to refer an issue to the manager.

When we talked about waiting on tables, we discussed the flow of a meal, beginning with the greeting, ordering the drinks, taking the entrée orders, and finally bringing the check. Just as a smoothly flowing meal service will make happy diners, a smoothly flowing shopping experience will lead to happy shoppers.

Look at the store from a customer's eyes. If a customer walks into your store, do they see a clean, well-lit shop? Can they immediately see the products that you're offering? Are there directions to help them orient themselves?

Ask yourself, "If I didn't already know where we keep the books on Julius Caesar (or light bulbs, or rutabagas), would I be able to find them quickly?" If the answer is no, then you need to rethink your signs.

There are those who will disagree with me on this point. Their plan is to have the customer ask a staff member, who then smiles a huge, friendly smile and leads them to the exact shelf. I dislike this plan for several reasons.

First, it assumes that the customer has come for one thing, and not several. Second, unless the store has almost no customers or else a huge number of employees, this model is not sustainable. It quickly becomes overloaded, and when it fails, it fails completely, as in the coffee shop story, above.

I once had an exceptionally bad experience in a hardware store that subscribed to this model of customer service. I was looking for a short length of solid 14AWG electrical wire. In this particular hardware store, they never sold pre-cut lengths of wire. One either purchased an entire spool of 100' or one had a piece cut to length.

Unfortunately, there was no one in the electrical department. I stopped an employee who was passing by, and asked to have the wire cut, but apparently it was the store's policy that only the salesperson in the electrical department was allowed to cut wire. I followed him to the threaded fastener aisle, where the person covering electrical was helping someone else. He was also holding a wireless phone to his ear, presumably to call another store in hopes that they would have what the customer needed.

I waved to him, pointed to the spool of wire that I had carried from the shelf in electrical, and then pointed to the electrical department. I meant to signal that when he was done, I needed for him to cut some wire. He glared at me and snapped, "I'm with a customer!"

Now, as you can see, the intended system of personal service with a smile, and maximum interaction between customers and store staff, had already broken down. The one person I needed was saturated with customers, and couldn't address my request.

I can even understand his frustration with the system that was overloading him, although he should have kept his calm, even under stress. The system was working against him, because the system was poorly designed, and set him up to fail.

Of course, this could have been avoided by having more staff who were allowed to cut wires, or by having someone else covering the threaded-fastener area.

In the end, I gave up and bought a length of #12 stranded that had apparently been cut for another customer, and then returned. It didn't work for what I needed. I went to a competing store, found a pre-cut length of #14 solid, and used that instead.

Because the system of having every customer personally guided to the required product is not a sustainable model, we need good signs and a store layout that makes sense. We need to design our service model around the customer being able to help themselves, or needing minimal assistance.

Returning to the flow of a customer shopping experience: The customer enters, the customer sees the desired product, and then the customer chooses the product. At this point, the customer is deciding if he needs a five-eighths or a nine-sixteenths plug, perhaps, or deciding if the display adapter on sale has the ports that will integrate with his existing monitor. If the customer needs help, he will ask. Be attentive, but not intrusive.

If the customer needs additional items, the system will repeat, or the customer may decide to browse for a while. Browsing is good, because it leads to the customer discovering additional items that he didn't know he needed. Browsing often leads to more sales.

Once the customer has everything, he will proceed to the register. Will he be able to get there? It seems like a silly question, until you see stores with the check stands only two to three feet from a prominent display. If the customer has nowhere to stand, he may decide that he doesn't need the product, and he may just leave. Also, if there's only one checker, the customer may simply decide not to wait.

If you are the checker, greet the customer politely. A simple "Hello" will usually suffice. "Good morning" is always appropriate, at least before noon. A good follow up question such as, "Did you find everything you needed today?" is always nice.

Smile, and be friendly, even if the customer is gruff and rude. Remember the ARES method. Remember that it's not about you – the guest is never mad at you; you just happen to be the nearest person. Smile and let it go.

Once the customer has been rung up, receive the payment graciously. As we discussed before, place the cash out of reach of the customer before making change. On the shelf above the cash drawer is a good spot. This way, if the customer says, "Hey, I gave you a twenty!" you can simply say, "This is the bill that you gave me, Sir."

This also prevents the guest from playing quick-change games and pocketing the money, at your expense.

When you give change, always give coins first. The coins go into the center of the palm. Bills go on top of coins. Last comes the receipt, if the customer wants a printed receipt. Some clerks will say the numbers as they give the change, such as "Your total is two-forty-one, plus fifty-nine makes three," as they give the coins, then "plus two makes five, and five is ten." You may need to practice it until you can say it smoothly, and only use it if it helps you to give change accurately and efficiently.

Please do not stack the bills on the receipt and then put the coins on top, like a paperweight. The customer will not be able to easily close his hand around that stack, and the coins will wind up spilling all over the counter. Coins first, bills second, receipt last (and only if desired).

Wait until the customer has gathered his things and started to move away before you start to ring up the next customer. This way, if the customer stops and asks a question, or points out that you've given him a Canadian quarter, you will not mix up the two orders, and the next guest won't run into him.

The next expected event is that the customer will leave the store, contented with his or her purchases.

At each stage of the customer's progress, you are meant to be their advocate, and an advocate for the store. Help the customer find and buy the product; help the store make sales.

By now you are probably starting to see that the same principles always apply, regardless where you are providing customer service.

Chapter 7
Setting Up Your Employees to Fail

AS I WRITE THIS, the COVID 19 disease is ravaging California. In our county, here, the public is currently required to wear masks when outside one's home, and most businesses which provide hot food and drink may sell items to go, and not for in-restaurant eating. Posted business hours just don't apply.

One of the allowed purposes for which the public may go abroad is for exercise. My habit, when possible, is to go for a long walk, arranging the midpoint to correspond with a coffee shop. This gives me a reward for my exercise – positive reinforcement – and also provides refreshment for the return trip.

The other day, while doing exactly that, I found myself about two miles from my car, but a few blocks from a coffee shop. I ordered a coffee using the online app, which showed that the coffee shop was open, and would receive my order promptly. So I slogged several blocks uphill, and well off my planned route, to reach this particular store.

On arrival, I found all the doors locked. There was a line at the drive-through, but the doors were locked. The door on the back of the store, accessible only from the parking lot, had signs indicating that walk-in pickup was available, but only from 7 AM to 11 AM. Since it was then nearly 1 PM, this did nothing to help me.

It wouldn't be safe to walk through the drive-up lane, and it there was no other means provided to access the workers in the store. There was no way to cancel the order in the app, nor could I use the app to signal the problem to the workers within. I had to knock at the door persistently until a worker came to the door and opened it to politely ask what I needed.

"I have a mobile order," I said.

"We only accept walk-up orders until 11 AM," she said, pointing to the hand-printed sign.

"Well, then you need to close your store in the app," I replied.

"We aren't in control of that," she answered. "But I'll go and get your order." Which she did, and timely.

In this event, we had a big thing that went wrong, and another big thing that went right.

What went wrong? Well, the app set up the workers at the store to fail. They accepted orders that could not be filled, given the limits on the store's walk-up hours. The app did not permit dialog with the store itself. The app did not allow the store to set its walk-up hours differently from the drive-through hours.

These are serious failings, because they led to moderately annoyed customers pounding on the door, trying to get the value for which they have already paid through the app. I suppose that I might possibly have tried calling my bank to demand that they reject the charge for the order, but it should not be my duty, as the customer, to reject the charge, or to fix the store's error.

But there was something that went very right. First of all, the worker responded to me. The workers could, justifiably, have ignored the crazy man pounding on the door. Or they might have called the police and stated that they were fearful for their safety. Odds are that the coffee store chain would have lost me as a customer, but those would have been justifiable actions on the part of the workers.

Second, she listened to me. She could have barked, "We're closed!" and slammed the door in my face. That would have been rude – but it happens sometimes, and with even less provocation. However, she listened to me, and acknowledged my complaint.

Third, as an advocate for the store, she explained the official position – that the hours ended at 11 AM, and that the workers had no control over the app's data. But as an advocate for me, the customer, she told me that she would get my order for me, and then she did so.

An included detail in that last sentence is that she made a promise – to get my drink – and fulfilled that promise. It is vitally important that you keep any promise that you make. It follows from that that you must be careful to only promise what you can deliver.

We've talked earlier about the things she did right, so let's talk about the thing that went wrong: The app accepted the order while the store was not configured to fulfill the order.

The workers in the store did not fail. They did exactly what they had been instructed to do. They operated as a walk-up for 4 hours, then converted to drive-up only. But that set of instructions set them up to fail. There were not going to be able to fulfill orders.

This is one example of a broader problem.

Suppose that you have a small restaurant and you want to have a marching band that marches among the tables, playing John Philip Souza's Stars and Stripes Forever. You have set up the restaurant to fail. The configuration of the business model makes the waiters' efforts fail. The cook might as well not be there at all; the guests will not have a pleasant meal, because they will not be able to think about their palates. They'll be too busy worrying about their ears.

You will have set up your employees to fail.

Suppose that you have a restaurant with a novel concept: A sit down menu, and also a do-it-yourself cupcake bar. So you intend to have couples sitting down to a romantic candlelit dinner, and next to them, children running back and forth with handfuls of frosting. That's a concept that just doesn't work. The main reason that it doesn't work is that neither set of customers – the diners or the cupcake eaters – will have a pleasant meal. The two sets of customers are mutually incompatible.

You will have set up your employees to fail.

Suppose that your small business has a single entrance door, and is arranged so that the customer standing at the cash register can literally block customers from walking in or out. I actually encountered this in a computer shop once; there was literally not room for more than one customer at a time in the store. If you do this, your business will definitely not succeed.

You will have set up your employees to fail.

I've seen each of those circumstances on real life – perhaps I'm exaggerating about the live music example – but as odd as it seems, people actually think that you can operate businesses that way. It never occurs to them to see the business as the customer sees it.

Suppose, for example, that your store is actually a maze, a mystery for the customer to solve, like an escape room in reverse. The customer, who merely wants to find a certain product, pay for it, and leave, must first decipher the trail of clues that you've artfully arranged.

I once tried to buy truffles for a photo shoot. I went to a popular local chocolatier where I was certain that I would find truffles for sale. The windows were completely covered with posters and banners, and were barely even translucent, but I could see that shadowy figures of people were clearly moving around inside. And front door was locked.

After a moment of scratching my head and looking for clues, I discovered the one hand-written paper sign, taped to the door among the various fliers and posters, that said to use the back door. So I walked down to the corner and down the side street.

Behind the row of shops there was a small obscure parking lot. It was not pedestrian-friendly. A slightly hidden back door from the parking lot had a small sign with the name of the shop on it. So I walked in and approached the candy counter.

There were several employees making candy, and several others behind the counter, packaging chocolates. None of them looked up or acknowledged me in any way. I looked through the selection on display and chose the candies that would work best for the photos.

Then I turned to a worker nearby.

"Excuse me," I said, "I'd like to buy a pound of these."

She looked up, startled, and stared at me in amazement. "How did you get in here?"

"The door was open," I said, pointing.

"Oh. We're closed on Wednesdays. That's supposed to be locked." She shrugged. "I guess I can sell you one pound."

So, having clarified that I had managed to find the hidden entrance, and that I hadn't somehow divined the strange secret schedule, which, of course, was not posted on the door where one would expect it to be – not that it could have been found among all the other papers posted on the door – Then, and only then, they consented to sell me chocolates.

They had set themselves up to fail. And I recently heard that they closed for lack of business. I wonder why, don't you?

So, let's generalize here: What do these disasters have in common? They fail to see the business from the customer's side.

Remember that you are the advocate for the customer. Your job is to guide the customer through the process. You start when the customer is approaching the door. The customer needs to understand how to access the business. Make it the most obvious possible route.

Assume that the customer knows nothing about the business or about how it operates. Assume that they are not going to figure out to go around to the back door, but only on days in June that start with a T.

It's not reasonable to ask that of your customers.

Notice your customers when they come in. If the door is supposed to be locked, don't leave it unlocked. If a customer does walk into your business while you're closed, notice them immediately, and say something along the lines of "Excuse me, I'm sorry, but we're closed today."

Don't just let them wander around looking at merchandise. It makes no sense to leave someone wandering around while you're closed. It's rude to the customer, it's dangerous for your employees, and it's just plain weird. And not in a good way.

Once the phantom customer attracts your attention, don't launch into an inquiry as to how they managed to breach your security perimeter. Don't wonder, out loud, how the customer didn't know that you're closed on Wednesdays. Assume that they didn't get the memo, and realize that it's your responsibility to clearly communicate your hours and your preferred business methods.

But most importantly, just wait on the customer.

As it happened, the chocolatier did sell me a pound of chocolates. And the truffles served the purpose well. I would actually be willing to go back and to try to decode the business method again in order to buy more chocolates, should the occasion arise.

Of course, now the occasion won't arise: They closed for lack of business. That's a stumper, isn't it?

We also set up employees to fail when don't give them the materials or the training to do their jobs. I remember a restaurant in this town ... it's under new management now ... where the servers were in the habit of walking quickly past a table and plunking plates down as they went by. Once, while I was eating there with friends, we had a saucer with three pickle slices suddenly plunked down in front of us.

We knew the people who would be taking over the restaurant in a few months, so we asked them about it. It turns out that there was once a custom at this restaurant of presenting each table with a relish tray, which was supposed to include a variety of small finger foods, such as vegetable slices, pickles, olives, and a few other savory items. It's on the order of an appetizer, and is meant to soften the wait for one's meal while providing a foretaste of the entrée to come.

Unfortunately, over time, the kitchen staff had stopped including one item or another. Perhaps there wasn't time to slice vegetables one evening. After a couple of weeks, omitting vegetables became the norm. One evening, at the last moment, someone realized that there were no olives in stock. The olives became the next omission. In the end, the relish tray diminished to three slices of pickle.

Remember when we talked about the fellow in the bowling alley who was ridiculously obsessed with the rule about outside food? Well, this rule – that all guests get a relish tray even if we only have pickle slices – was another example of a rule that could be ignored once in a while. The purpose of the rule was no longer being met.

Along the same line, I once stayed in a certain hotel on the East Coast, which was affiliated with the hotel in which I worked. I checked into my room, and about half an hour later, there was a knock at the door. A sheepish bellman handed me a small metal bowl and said, "From the management." In the bowl there was a small orange, a spotty apple, and a slightly lumpy grapefruit.

He hastily retreated, leaving me holding the bowl.

I had to scratch my head over that one for a while, before realizing that in some manual, somewhere, there was likely an instruction that probably said, "Fellow employees from hotels in our group are to be greeted with a fruit basket," or something along those lines. The small metal bowl, with these three hastily selected fruits, was the very loose interpretation of that rule, after many prior improvisations.

Once again, the purpose of the rule was no longer being met.

Honestly, I found both situations slightly amusing, and slightly sad. These well-intentioned flourishes of guest service failed, not because the employees didn't care, but because the employees didn't have what they needed to succeed.

I didn't need a relish tray. My friends and I would not have missed it had it not been there. But had it been done well, with a variety of tasty nibbles to stave off starvation pending the entrée, then it would have been a nice touch. The employees lacked the resources to do that, and they lacked the authority to fix the problem. A manager or shift lead that was paying attention to what was happening would have either fortified the relish tray, or skipped it altogether.

In the same way, I didn't expect a fruit basket. I thought it was quite generous of the hotel company to give me the complimentary room-night. But if the managers intended to follow a policy regarding fruit baskets, then the proper thing to do would have been to order a bona-fide fruit basket ahead of time. As it was, I imagined some harried front desk supervisor turning to a bellman and saying, "Oh, look! This fellow works for us! He's supposed to get a fruit basket! Quick, go to the kitchen, put some fruit in a bowl, and take it up to his room."

Honestly, at that point, it would have been better to skip it entirely. But it is the management, who made a policy, without giving the necessary material resources, the training, and the ongoing guidance, who made this a customer-service failure. They set up their staff to fail.

One other example comes to mind of a good policy gone bad. Two friends and I walked into a pizza place, intending to place an order to go. We'll call it Perfect Pizza.

There were two employees behind the counter. As we walked in, the first employee faced each of us in turn and said, "Welcome to Perfect Pizza, can I help you? Welcome to Perfect Pizza, can I help you? Welcome to perfect Pizza, can I help you?"

Right behind him, and slightly out of sync, almost like "Row, row, row your boat," the second employee faced each of us in turn and said the same litany: "Welcome to Perfect Pizza can I help you welcome to Perfect Pizza can I help you welcome to Perfect Pizza can I help you?"

We chuckled slightly at the odd recital, and asked a question about one of the pizzas. The employee to whom we asked the question called out for help to a third employee, who was in the back. She immediately popped through the doorway and said, "Welcome to Perfect Pizza can I help you welcome to Perfect Pizza can I help you welcome to Perfect Pizza can I help you?"

It was a good idea: Greet every customer who walks in with a welcome and an offer to help. Unfortunately, it fell through in the execution. A well-intentioned corporate officer must have written the policy. It probably said, "Every guest is to be greeted upon entry with this phrase…"

A well-intentioned manager must have drilled the employees on exactly what to say every time anyone walks through the door. Corporate policy says X, every person who walks through the door could be a secret corporate test visitor, so always do X.

Perhaps the shift leads even held the employees responsible for following the precise litany every single time: "I learned to do it exactly like this, so you need to learn to do exactly like this."

Honestly, since we were all together, one greeting from one employee would have been fine. Six identical greetings were a few too many, and seemed a bit odd; the last three greetings really seemed comical. A bit of common sense could have made it a nice touch instead of a really bizarre touch.

I do understand how it happened. It is much easier to train someone to do exactly X when they see exactly Y than to ask them to follow a more complex rule. "If someone walks in the door, immediately say this, every time," is a very simple rule and is very easy to understand.

A better system would be to have the first employee to see the guests greet each group of guests. It takes a bit more training, and the employee has to realize that it is or is not his turn to greet the customers. The employee has to use judgement to tell which customers are together and which are from a different group.

But the end result will be better.

Nine greetings instead of one is not a major problem. It didn't make us swear off pizza, or vow never to return. In fact, we were slightly amused by it, though we were careful not to laugh in front of the employees.

Nonetheless, it's a well-intentioned rule that was applied too thickly, and made the company seem less professional instead of more professional. It wasn't quite a setup for failure, but it could have been a setup for some exasperated employee to decide that the rule was completely ridiculous, and instead greet customers with "Whaddaya want?" or "Fearer Tagoe!"

We definitely don't want to exasperate the employees into wholesale rebellion. Remember your first job. Remember the things you had to learn, and the rules you had to follow. Based on those memories, try to set rules that make sense, and give people the leeway to use those rules appropriately.

I realize that many of my examples pertain to food. I think that it's because we most often see good and bad examples of customer service in restaurant settings. But failures on a massive scale can be anywhere.

I once spent several hours trying to order electronics from a website that very clearly showed the entire line of merchandise offered by the company, with excellent detail and specific specifications. And no shopping cart.

There weren't even any prices. I could clearly see that they offered patch cables in five sizes and twelve colors. I couldn't have bought a single one of them to save my life. It was like a store with no front door.

I finally emailed the webmaster and pointed out how useless the site was, and how it wasted my time and his bandwidth to even have such a business online. In retrospect, even though it was frustrating, that might have been an over-reaction.

He answered, deeply offended, and told me that the information on the website was for the potential investors. Well, I personally don't see why people would invest in a business that can't actually make money by actually selling things. But maybe there's an investment strategy that consists of buying stocks that will fail. What do I know?

That corporation, needless to say, set itself up to fail.

I once went into a major hardware chain on a Saturday. I just needed a few small things, but there was one register working, and there was a line of customers that went down the aisle for the entire length of the store. It seems that a couple of the register operators had called in sick, and the managers hadn't done anything about it.

My question was this: Why didn't some of the management and floor staff – and there were plenty of them around – simply open a few registers themselves? The single most critical part of the sales process is accepting the customer's money. When people are lined up across the store hoping to give you money, and you can't be bothered to take it, you have set up your workers to fail.

A coworker and I once went to Dallas to install a phone system. There was a fast food chain there that we wanted to try, but it would be a long working day for us, so we drove by early in the morning to see what hours they were open. A hand printed sign in the window read: *Hours: 10 AM till closing*.

That was a failure for two reasons. First, no sign in your business should EVER be hand-printed. We live in the 21st century, after all. We have computers and printers. But most importantly, saying that you will be open until you close gives no useful information to the customer. You know what time you close, but the customer can't possibly know until you tell him.

Tip: Customers will not read your mind. They simply refuse to know things that you do not tell them.

I have to think that maybe there was not a set time for closing, and the sign meant to convey that they would be open from 10 AM until they sold out of whatever they sell. In that case, it should have said *Hours: 10 AM till Sold Out*. While still very indeterminate, it would at least give something useful to the customer.

But the hand lettered sign, as we found it, merely set up the store for failure. Small failure – most customers would probably be able to visit the store during the hours that it was open, whatever those might be.

But it was still a setup for failure.

So how do you set up your business to succeed?

Well, you make the customer comfortable walking in the front door. You remove obstacles that would prevent easy access to your business. You make it obvious how to obtain what the customer came for. You avoid obscure and inscrutable methods. You see the business with the customer's eyes. You make the experience pleasant for the customer.

You should also arrange some sort of spot check, in the form of trusted persons who call your business, or walk into your business, and makes a list of things that seem weird, or unpleasant, or that interfere with their shopping experience.

You can do telephone audits fairly easily. Simply call, or have a friend call, and follow a script. See if the person answering the phone follows the set procedure.

It is a bit more difficult to audit retail store performance. You can have people you know walk in, but it won't take long for them to be recognized by the staff. Comment cards, follow-up emails, and electronic surveys can help.

In a restaurant, the manager or a representative should eat a meal during business hours at least once a month. I used to know a manager who ate lunch every day in a restaurant that was only open for dinner. The problem with his strategy is that the one lunch did not represent the performance of the kitchen and dining room during an actual meal.

If you want your employees not to fail, what are some things you can do to set them on the right foot? First, see the business from the customer's eyes, and use test customers if necessary. Secondly, set policies that make sense, and train your people to use those policies wisely. Third, have a professional environment that does not overload your staff. Fourth, don't make the customer think. Everything that the customer needs to know should be obvious to a random stranger.

Chapter 8
Telephones and Call Centers.

"GOOD MORNING AND THANK you for calling."

That's a good way to start a telephone conversation. Of course, no book on customer service would be complete if we didn't talk about telephones. Some of your customers will call you from time to time. They deserve the same good service that they would enjoy if they were sitting in front of you, across a counter, at a desk, or at a table.

When answering a phone for a business, it's good to have a short script that you keep in your head, so that you will automatically say the right words each time. Some businesses have templates for their telephone greetings. I recommend that you create a script and memorize it. This will keep you from suddenly realizing that you don't know what to say after you've picked up the phone.

Here are some samples, if your business does not already have a standard template:

"Thank you for calling the Chein-Verte Inn. How may I direct your call?"

"Good morning from the Chein-Verte Inn. May I place you on a brief hold?"

"Happy holidays, and thank you for calling. This is Susie. How may I assist you?"

In telling you about telephone etiquette, I do have to remark that not everyone feels the need for a verbose greeting. One of my long-time colleagues in the hotel business always answered every call with a polite, "This is Dave." It seemed to work for him, and no one ever complained that he had been rude. Still, if you're not Dave, I recommend that you have a polite phrase that rolls easily off of your tongue.

Personally, I avoid time-related phrases such as "good morning" or "good afternoon," as these change with the time of day. You may not notice that it's now twelve-thirty, but your guest will be a bit taken aback if you wish her a good morning when it's no longer morning.

Like nearly everything else about customer service, you can find the right thing to do by asking what you would expect if you were the customer. Would you expect someone to pick up the phone and say, "Whaddaya Want?" No? Then don't do that.

I sometimes call businesses and hear an employee say something unintelligible. You may know that " 'Lo, ChenVerInn?" means "Hello, [this is the] Chein Verte Inn, [how may I help you]?" but your customer will not. So don't do that.

It is especially important to speak clearly and completely when speaking to someone for whom English is not the first language. As hospitality professionals and customer service professionals, we are likely to meet people from all over the globe.

Many of them will not understand English, or will understand it poorly. If you slur your words, or use slang, insider terms, or kitchen jargon, they will not understand you. When possible, make sure that the person to whom you are speaking understands you. If necessary, repeat the phrase a different way.

If you need to put someone on hold, or transfer a call, always ask for and receive the caller's consent. Even if it's 4:55 PM, and you are dying to get out the door, you must still ask for the caller's consent before transferring the caller.

If there are a large number of calls that you consistently transfer to the same place, such as a reservations line, ask your telecom provider about a speed dial for that number. I like to use #* as a feature code for speed dial, and then have speed dial code 1 point to reservations. This way, a busy front desk clerk just needs to touch three corners of the keypad to send the call to reservations.

After, of course, the caller consents to be transferred.

Suppose that you are the only front desk clerk working at a hotel. A guest comes up to the front desk, and begins to ask about dinner reservations. A moment later, the phone rings. What should you do?

The correct answer is to say, "Pardon me for one moment," to the guest at the counter, answer the phone, and say, "Thank you for calling. May I please place you on a brief hold?" Then, in a perfect world, you would then serve the customer at the counter, followed by the customer on the phone.

What if the customer will not consent to hold?

In that case, offer to take the caller's number and return the call. If the caller still declines, find out what the customer on the phone needs. It might be an emergency, so the caller may have a good reason to speak to you at once. Or they may have been transferred to wrong numbers by other hotels, and may not trust you to recover the call.

Your hotel or business may have a policy on this as well, and of course that policy will override anything that is in this book.

If the caller says, "Reservations, please," your response should be "Certainly, Sir," and then to transfer the call to *#1, or whatever speed dial code you use. As with speaking to customers in person, from chapter one of this book, always be polite, and use titles whenever appropriate.

If you place a caller on hold, either retrieve the call promptly, or have a coworker pick up the call as soon as possible. Placing the customer on hold is making a promise to pick up that call quickly. Always keep your promises to a guest.

Always end a telephone conversation with a polite closing, such as "Thanks again for calling. Goodbye."

I had a very bad telephone experience with a certain service company once. I was calling to verify details of a transaction, and it appears that I caught them about thirty minutes before closing. As soon as I explained what I wanted, the attendant transferred my call to the right desk, and I got a voicemail box.

I called back and got the same attendant. I explained that the person had already left, and that I needed to speak to a live person. Could she verify that someone was there to take the call before transferring me?

She certainly could, and she transferred me to a live person, who answered the phone ... and who cut me off in mid-sentence to transfer me to the original voicemail box. When I called back the third time, the attendant didn't bother to answer.

What should have happened? Well, the attendant should never have blind-transferred a call (that's when you transfer a call before the other person answers). It is acceptable to say, "The person you need isn't in, and I don't believe that anyone else can answer that question for you. Would you like her voicemail?"

But it is not acceptable to transfer a call into limbo.

The second person who answered should have let me finish my request, at the very least. Then, she could have said, "I'm sorry, but the only person who can answer that question has already left for the day. Would you like her voicemail?"

It goes without saying, mainly because we've already said it so many times, but on a telephone, as in any other area of customer service, think about how you wish to be treated, and treat the caller accordingly.

Of course, in the modern age, telephones are no longer the main means of communication. Email and texting also demand good manners. You may be in the habit of sending your friends cryptic messages such as "Ware RU," but any message you send from a business needs to be businesslike. "Your table at the Chein-Verte Diner is now ready" is an acceptable text. "UR nXt" is not.

Three main rules should apply:

1. Use complete sentences.
2. Spell out the words.
3. Say the business name so that the guest knows who it's from.

Those same rules apply to emails, also. Address the guest formally, state the matter at hand in full sentences, avoid jargon, spell words properly, and say who it's from.

Should you have occasion to respond to an online review or comment card, these same rules apply, and you must also remember to remain calm. It's not about you. Use the ARES method, from chapter 5.

Your business most likely has a designated person who responds to online reviews or comments, and if you are that person, be sure to follow your business' policy. Even if there is no policy, remember to remain professional at all times.

Suppose that a customer stated, in an online review, that they had a horrible time, that the reservationist was rude, and that the curtains smelled like popcorn. You might be tempted to write a scathing denial, and call the person a fake guest, or say something along that line.

Don't do it.

Instead, a reply that says, "We're terribly sorry that you didn't enjoy your stay. We have discussed the cleanliness of the curtains with our housekeeping manager, and we have reviewed your reservation as well. We hope that you will change your mind, and stay with us again," would be much better.

First, the gentle answer contradicts the claim that the reservationist was rude. If someone was rude to the guest, readers of the review can see that it wasn't the normal experience.

Second, the response addresses the guest's specific issues, and describes positive steps taken to make things better.

Third, inviting someone back, even someone rude who has said the most horrible things online about your business, gives you the high ground.

A rude and sarcastic reply might feel good, and it might even be wickedly funny, but it will not help the reputation of the business. In the long run, sarcasm and rudeness will always work against you.

Remember, it costs you nothing to apologize. It costs you nothing at all to be polite. Do not accept responsibility or liability, of course. But be polite. Note the phrase, "We're terribly sorry that you didn't enjoy your stay." It apologizes for the one thing that is definitely true: This guest did not enjoy his stay. If you offer a remedy, as the policies of your business will determine, make sure that it is an appropriate remedy for the issue.

Radios are also commonly used in many businesses, including hotels. As with any communication, a professional attitude is needed. Do not use slang or jargon.

When speaking on a telephone, or writing an email, you can have fairly good confidence that you know who will receive the message. With radio, you do not. Radios are not limited to your specific business.

For this reason, I recommend simple radio codes. A set of ten codes, specific to your business, is one way to accomplish this. Of course, some of the standard 10 codes will work, such as 10-4 for yes, okay, or will do. In addition to those, you will want other codes specific to the issues that your business faces.

One business that I know of used a series of codes that began with code 10 (an issue involving a guestroom toilet), and went through code 11 (an issue involving an elevator), up to code 14, a problem reported by a certain manager.

With radio, always assume that the guests can hear everything that you say over the airwaves.

Imagine that you are a guest in a hotel and you happen to be near a gardener who has turned up his radio far too loud. You suddenly hear a calm voice saying, "Code 17, main lobby, back entrance." You will think nothing of it, except perhaps, "That man should either turn down his radio or wear an earpiece."

But if you were to hear, "Hey, there's some weird guy by the back entrance of the lobby, he looks like he might be drunk, can security go check it out?" then you're going to be a bit concerned that maybe you've chosen the wrong hotel. That's not the impression that you want to give your customers, and, as we all know, incidents like that do arise, even in the best establishments.

For that matter, imagine if you were to overhear, "Hey, Joe, this guest in room 228 is being a royal pain. Can you go see what the hell he wants this time?" How would you feel about the professionalism and customer service skills of the hotel staff?

A better and more professional approach would be to say, "Unit 3, please see the guest at room 228 for an unknown request." That would be professional, and would not embarrass the guest if his family were to overhear it on someone's radio.

Our goal in keeping radio communications professional is to keep from making incidents worse. Any angry guest, who has been rudely and dismissively addressed over the radio, will be angrier than before. A guest who hears about suspicious people lurking outside the hotel will be alarmed and will worry about his safety.

Radio transmissions need to be discrete, simple, and use agreed-upon codes whenever possible. Radio users need to be sensitive to the guests around them, and should turn radios down, or off, while in guest areas or in places where radios might be overheard.

Call centers, such as a hotel's reservation center, deserve a bit of attention. In a call center, a group of people, called "Agents," are given calls based on which of them has been idle the longest. The calls come into a central number, called the pilot number, and are then held in a queue until someone is available to take the call. Calls that wait too long will be pushed out of the que to an overflow number.

If you do not answer the phone when it is your turn, the call will return to the queue, and your phone will be placed in a not-ready state. You will not get any more calls until you make yourself ready again.

When a caller calls into a call center, what are the caller's expectations? Most likely, the caller wishes to be connected quickly, and to handle whatever caused them to call you. You can help by answers calls when they come to you, and giving them your full attention. Don't let calls drop back into the queue, and try to handle calls efficiently, so that callers don't overflow out of the queue.

As always with phones, have a script. Plan what you will say to various questions. Be ready for angry customers. Remember ARES.

Guest service with telephones, electronics, and radios is really just the same set of guest service concepts, applied in a different way. Be polite, do not mirror what you see in front of you, and maintain a patient, gentle attitude. Remember that it's not about you. Use polite words, full sentences, and remain calm at all times. Make the guest's experience something that will inspire them to write a complimentary letter to your manager.

With telephones, always use a script that you have memorized. Get permission from the caller before transferring or placing a caller on hold. Give priority to the guest who is in front of you, ahead of telephone callers. In emails, use proper spelling and complete sentences. Use the same formal language that you would use with a guest in person: Please, Thank You, Ma'am, Sir.

On the radio, be polite, and use formal radio protocol, including codes for any sensitive topics. Never speak about a guest by name over a radio, and be respectful at all times.

What Have We Learned?

Let's review the high points of the lessons in this book, to make sure that we always provide good customer service.

The three undeniable rules of customer service:

1. Customers like good service.
2. Customers will pay for good service.
3. Customers will return if they get good service.

The four rules for speaking to customers:

RULE 1: A customer is always "Sir" or "Madam." Whenever one speaks to a guest one always says "Yes, Sir," or "Yes, Ma'am," or the equivalent.

RULE 2: "Please" and "Thank you" are mandatory.

RULE 3: There are no problems. Say "My pleasure," instead.

RULE 4: Your tone is as important as your words.

How to Be the Perfect Table Waiter:

1. Make the customer feel welcome.
2. Be friendly without being familiar.
3. Be attentive without being intrusive.
4. Don't vanish.
5. Always step into the customer's field of vision before speaking.

How to Address Customers at a Table:

Approach and be seen.
Before speaking, wait for a pause.
Casually ask any question that you may have.

Understand the Stages of a Meal:

1. Guest is seated.
2. Drink orders.
3. Entree orders.
4. Food is served.
5. Dessert is offered.
6. The check is given and paid.

Your Role as a Customer Service Professional:

Be an advocate for the business to the customer, and
Be an advocate for the customer to the business.

TIP: Don't use jargon with customers.
TIP: Understand when the customer is not right, but be friendly and polite anyway.

© LCR 2021

Rules of Making Things Right:

1. Follow the standards and policies set by your manager.
2. A remedy must be of the same scale as the offense.
3. Offer a choice of solutions or remedies.

How to know if you're offering an appropriate remedy:

1. Are you being friendly in tone and polite in your speech?
2. Is what you're offering reasonable? Is the product you're selling worth the price you're asking?
3. Is the remedy you're offering the right size for the issue that you're trying to correct?
4. Would you be satisfied with the remedy that you are offering?

Key slogan: "Don't give away the hotel."

TIP: Beware of fast-change artists.
TIP: Give change: coins first, bills second.
TIP: Never promise something that you can't deliver.
TIP: Keep any promise that you make.

Rules for a professional environment:

1. Don't lounge in the customer areas.
2. Keep background music in the background.
3. Forget about live music.

When the customer is angry, use ARES

© LCR 2021

    Attitude – Remain calm; it's not about you.
    Reaction – Do not react; help dampen the guest's reaction.
    Expectations – Find out what the guest expected.
    Solutions – Provide a choice of two or more solutions, within reason.

TIP: Don't claim responsibility or liability.
TIP: When you are the customer, try to tip.
TIP: Never expect or ask for a tip.

For Managers and Owners:
How not to set up your employees to fail:

1. Make it clear whether you are open and taking orders, or closed.
2. Make it clear how to do business with you.
3. Empower employees to help the customers do business with you.
4. Forget about live music.
5. Think about your business from a customer's perspective.
6. Maintain good flow paths for customers to come in and go out.
7. Provide the things, the training, and the guidance to help your staff follow the policies that you set in place.
8. Think of yourself as an advocate for the customer.

TIP: Customers will not read your mind. They simply refuse to know things that you do not tell them.

Would you like more copies of this book for your business?

You can buy additional copies at Lulu.com
(Search by Title or Author)

Or contact Rock and Fire Press:

Rock and Fire Press
Customer Service Department
337 E. Laurel Drive
Salinas, CA 93906

www.ingramcontent.com/pod-product-compliance
Lightning Source LLC
Chambersburg PA
CBHW031418040426
42444CB00005B/623